More Praise for *Tak*

In *Taking Back the Vote,* Eisner asks the hard question—how can we truly embed voting in our culture? And she provides very compelling answers—among them, show young people why voting matters in their own lives and make voting a celebrated ritual. Volunteering is way up in America; now is the time to systematically reengage Americans in the basic, democratic act of voting. Eisner's engaging book offers powerful and fresh ideas that help point the way.

—JOHN M. BRIDGELAND, PRESIDENT AND
CEO OF CIVIC ENTERPRISES AND FORMER
DIRECTOR OF USA FREEDOM CORPS

Taking Back the Vote is both sobering and inspiring for those of us who are striving to instill an appreciation of our democracy in the youth of today. Jane Eisner validates the belief I think we all hold that civic education and engagement can make a difference, and she manages to give the subject the urgency it deserves. Her discussion of the need to put political involvement side by side with community service as valued activities in our schools is provocative and worthy of study. Her ideas and the stories she relates are nothing less than a call to action. This book is must reading for everyone who cares about "keeping" the Republic, as Ben Franklin put it.

—JUDGE MARJORIE O. RENDELL,
FIRST LADY OF PENNSYLVANIA

Taking Back the Vote is more than an important practical guide to getting American youth involved in our democracy. This lively, fast-reading little book is an informative, passionate and persuasive argument in the tradition of the best American public debate. It should be read alongside the Federalist Papers' case for the ratification of the Constitution. Our eighteenth-century founders saw active-duty citizens as the key to successful self-government. Jane Eisner points the way for twenty-first-century Americans to make that hope come true.

—HARRIS WOFFORD, FORMER U.S. SENATOR AND CO-CHAIR
OF AMERICA'S PROMISE: THE ALLIANCE FOR YOUTH

TAKING BACK THE VOTE:

Getting American Youth Involved
in Our Democracy

JANE EISNER

Beacon Press
Boston

BEACON PRESS
25 Beacon Street
Boston, Massachusetts 02108-2892
www.beacon.org

Beacon Press books
are published under the auspices of
the Unitarian Universalist Association of Congregations.

07 06 05 04 8 7 6 5 4 3 2 1

This book is printed on acid-free paper that meets the uncoated paper
ANSI/NISO specifications for permanence as revised in 1992.

Composition by Wilsted & Taylor Publishing Services

LIBRARY OF CONGRESS CATALOGING-IN-PUBLICATION DATA

Eisner, Jane.
  Taking back the vote : getting American youth involved
in our democracy / Jane Eisner.— 1st pbk. ed.
p. cm.
  Includes bibliographical references.
  ISBN 0-8070-4343-5 (pbk. : alk. paper)
  1. Youth—United States—Political activity.
2. Voting—United States. I. Title.
HQ799.2.P6E37 2004
305.235'0973—dc22

                                        2004004641

TO RACHEL, AMALIA, AND MIRIAM

Contents

Prologue

This book began with a small, personal epiphany. It occurred on May 21, 2002, a brisk Tuesday, when voters across Pennsylvania were asked to select their party's nominee for governor and a few other important public offices. My oldest child had turned eighteen several months earlier and had registered to vote when she received her driver's license. This was to be her First Vote.

In our suburb outside Philadelphia, we vote in a century-old Scout House a short walk from our home, and I look forward to the ritual as I would a chance to have coffee and conversation with a good friend I see only twice a year. There's something pleasantly anachronistic about the routine—traipsing through the crunchy leaves of a neighbor's backyard in November or over the moist ground cover in May to a slightly shabby building staffed by well-meaning, if sometimes lonely-looking, volunteers. When my children were little, I'd bring along enough leftover Halloween candy to keep them quiet if the lines were long, but usually it wasn't necessary because some goodhearted soul had brought along her own basket of treats. As they grew into teenagers, it became harder to corral them into attendance, so I'd go alone, half-hoping to bump into a neighbor or campaigning candidate of my acquaintance. Voting is a social act, after all.

I had looked forward to that Tuesday in May with anticipation. Eager to mark the occasion for my daughter, I queried some thoughtful advisers for suggestions of a book I could give her, and once I fixed on the right one, rushed to the bookstore the night before to purchase it. I envisioned the next morning as a sort of Frank Capra moment—the walk to the polling place before school and work, the gift, the passing down of civic tradition from the daughter of immigrants to the granddaughter.

Of course, nothing goes as planned with teenagers. Running late, ankle hurt, she asked, Why can't we just drive, Mom? She smiled politely when I gave her the slim book of Walt Whitman poetry, bound in paper soft to the touch, but I don't think she cracked it open. Truth is, at that hour of the morning, I was simply glad that she was awake.

I didn't expect a demonstration of joy from her. No, the epiphany came afterward, when I realized that no one else seemed to care, either. Oh, the poll workers, bless them, clapped when they heard this was her first time voting, but in every other respect this significant civic milestone went largely unnoticed. We greet other rites of passage in our children's lives with great fanfare, videotaping the first step for posterity, spending hundreds on prom dresses and thousands on bar mitzvah parties, attending every soccer game and dance recital, swooning over the first date and swearing over the first car. Still, even in my well-organized, civic-minded neighborhood, my daughter's First Vote, her central act of citizenship, was welcomed by little more than a collective yawn.

From my work as an editor and then a columnist for the *Philadelphia Inquirer,* I was familiar with the growing body of research and literature detailing the decline of civic life in America, with voting (and newspaper reading) among the chief pieces of evidence. I had also extensively covered the promise and pitfalls of the burgeoning national service movement, both because I believed in how it could help server and recipient, and because I shared the hope that direct experience with social need would prompt more young people to vote and become politically engaged. Certainly my daughter was raised on those values, growing up in a household that vied for the newspaper over breakfast and schlepped to volunteer in soup kitchens and to participate in park clean-ups. At the moment of her First Vote, during her last academic quarter of high school, she was volunteering four days a week as a teacher's helper in a gritty, overcrowded public school in Philadelphia.

Unfortunately, no one was connecting the dots, for her or her peers. No one was guiding her to understand that the deplorable condition of the school where she volunteered was connected to the gubernatorial election, and that major decisions on education policy and funding affecting the kids she served every day would be made in Harrisburg and Washington by the people she had a chance to elect. Politicians don't talk to her generation, don't advertise on her television programs or call in to her radio stations. Schools aren't equipped to host that sort of civic lesson. Small wonder that she probably voted more to humor me than out of studied conviction. If so, she was only reflecting the behavior of her generation, who are voting at record lows, disengaged from politics and directing their considerable civic energy away from government and toward the fleeting gratification earned by volunteer work.

This book is aimed to give my daughter and her peers a reason to vote. It is also written for parents, educators, clergy, coaches—all who care about the next generation—to inform, inspire, agitate, jump-start a debate, and prod action on what I believe is the hottest civic issue of our time. While declining civic participation among young people is a trend afflicting many of the world's democracies, it is not immune to remedy; good people and good programs have proved that they can make a difference. In America, the moment for this discussion is ripe—as the national electorate remains evenly split, the untapped youth vote could have a profound impact on the status quo. "Campus kids can be the key swing group of the 2004 elections if the campaigns and the candidates for office properly engage them," predicted Dan Glickman, the former U.S. agriculture secretary who is now director of the Institute of Politics at Harvard's John F. Kennedy School of Government.

This historical trend of declining voting and political participation can be reversed. No longer is the civic challenge to expand the franchise, it is to *use* the franchise—recognize its worth and potential, and invite the next generation into the process.

It's the least my generation can do. After all, we who came of age during the raucous sixties—or, in my case, a few years later—have bequeathed this mess to our children. We are the ones who, over time, stopped voting and stopped caring, turning cynicism of public life into an art form and shopping into the highest form of civic duty. Consider this book a gift, a small down payment on the larger debt owed by a neglectful generation to its more hopeful progeny.

"I hear America singing," Walt Whitman wrote in the slim volume I gave my daughter on the day of her First Vote. I have no illusions that fifteen minutes in a voting booth will mark a turning point in a young life. But I hope that one day she'll open the pages of this extraordinary celebration of American life and understand the connection. When Whitman heard the "varied carols" of America singing—the mechanics and masons, shoemakers and sewers, "singing with open mouths their strong melodious songs"—I am certain he heard the sounds of a people who cared enough about their destiny to spend a few minutes once or twice a year in a voting booth and to pass along that value to their children.

CHAPTER ONE

No Longer Spectators:
The future is in their hands

At 10:05 A.M. on May 14, 1968, Senator Birch Bayh, a Democrat from Indiana, banged the gavel to open a congressional hearing that he believed would do nothing less than transform American political life. His was an urgent cause. Outside of this seat of power and many others, young people were taking to the streets to angrily protest war, economic policy, and the painful way modern societies were failing them. Earlier that week, a nationwide "March of the Poor" had reached Washington, while students and police battled each other in Paris. Only a month earlier, the Rev. Martin Luther King Jr.'s assassination was followed by violent riots in 130 American cities.

"In almost every aspect of American life today, there is discontent with the status quo," Bayh said in his introductory remarks. Nothing, he added, "is more fundamental or more directly related to the temper of our times than the effort upon which we embark today."

On that Tuesday, placed before the Subcommittee on Constitutional Amendments of the Committee on the Judiciary were three resolutions with much the same intent: to amend the Constitution to extend voting rights to citizens eighteen years of age or older.

Twenty-one was then the minimum age at which one could cast a ballot according to federal law, but already two states—Georgia and Kentucky—had granted the franchise to eighteen-year-olds. In Alaska, nineteen-year-olds could vote. In Hawaii, the voting age was twenty. At the moment Bayh's subcom-

2 NO LONGER SPECTATORS

mittee was convening in room G-308 in the New Senate Office Building, the state of Maryland was considering a constitutional amendment to lower the voting age to nineteen.

Change was in the air. Desperation, also. While Bayh noted that his Senate colleagues often despaired of the "docile, passive, and uninvolved attitude of the college generation of the 1950s," this generation was aching to get involved. As the senator noted, with hope and not a little anxiety:

No longer are young Americans content to sit idly by and watch the passing scene from the grandstand. They want to be down on the field. They have made it abundantly clear that they intend to participate in the game. No longer should older Americans be content to leave this vigorous and exciting force on the sidelines. This force, this energy, is going to continue to build and grow. The only question is whether we should ignore it, perhaps leaving this energy to dam up and burst and follow less-than-wholesome channels, or whether we should let this force be utilized by society through the pressure valve of the franchise.

This force, as Bayh called it, was 10.8 million strong. Americans who were eighteen, nineteen, and twenty years old comprised 5.5 percent of the population. As speaker after speaker would proudly note that day, these young people held high school degrees in record numbers, attended college in record numbers, and were far more educated and worldly than previous generations.

And, if they were men, they were also being drafted to fight an increasingly unpopular war in the rice paddies and jungles of Vietnam.

The connection to the war was undeniable: The notion that eighteen-year-olds were old enough to fight and die but not old enough to cast a ballot struck many in the room that day as too blatantly unfair to stomach anymore. Throughout American history, war has been a central motivation in extending the right to vote, whether to newly free blacks or working people who owned no property. As General William Tecumseh Sherman himself noted at the end of the Civil War, "When the fight is over, the hand that drops the musket cannot be denied the ballot."

But there was something else at work behind expanding the franchise this one last time. Not just fairness, and not just fear that without access to the voting booth young people would seek to change American society in more threatening ways. There was also a palpable belief that these new voters would improve the political system with their intelligence, idealism, and energy.

"The future, to repeat a truism, is in their hands," Senate Majority Leader Michael J. Mansfield, a Montana Democrat, said that day. "If it is to be a better nation and a better world—and I'm confident that it will be—the youth of today will make it so. I think the time is long overdue when they should be given more in the way of recognition, more in the way of public responsibility. . . . I am sure the contribution will be significant."

It would take another three years of hearings, lawsuits, and voter referenda before the Twenty-sixth Amendment was approved and eighteen-, nineteen-, and twenty-year-olds were allowed to vote in a presidential election. When Ohio became the thirty-eighth state to ratify the new amendment, the ideal of adult universal suffrage which long had tugged at the American conscience was essentially fulfilled. After centuries of struggle, we were finally a complete democracy. Those who had been forced to stand on the sidelines were now, to follow Birch Bayh's thought, set to rush the playing field and join the game.

But this game was over almost before it began.

The hoped-for surge of young people into the electoral process, with all the attendant reforms and improvements they would bring, has not happened in the three decades since. Instead, the participation of eighteen- to twenty-year-olds in the 1972 presidential election turned out to be the high point of their electoral involvement. With one exception (the presidential election of 1992), voter turnout among young people has, literally, been downhill ever since.

This is a trend like no other in the history of American suffrage. When other formerly disenfranchised groups were given the right to vote—such as women and blacks—their participation levels increased over time. At first after they won the right to vote in 1920, women went to the polls at a lower rate than men did. Now, women are more than half the voting electorate. The trend for youth voting goes in reverse. In 1972, 49.6 percent of the nation's eighteen- to twenty-four-year-olds voted; the percentage dropped to a third with the razor-thin race between George W. Bush and Al Gore in 2000. As for eighteen-year-olds that year, only 26.7 percent—barely more than just one out of every four—said they voted.

And though it's true that voting rates in all age groups have declined, youth voting has taken a much steeper path downward. By one measurement, overall turnout in presidential elections dropped 4 percent since 1972, but among eighteen- to twenty-five-year-olds, the drop was 15 percent. This despite the fact that young people today are the most educated generation America has ever had, and education once was a trusted predictor of voting behavior.   .

Yet these young people are not simply taking the ball and going home; they are redirecting their talents and energy to an entirely different game. Since childhood, this Millennial Generation, as the demographers Neil Howe and William Strauss dub them, has been steeped in the values of cooperation, teamwork, and service. In *Millennials Rising*, a compilation of research on the attitudes and behavior of Americans born since

1982, Howe and Strauss describe a generation more tolerant of racial diversity, more attuned to "girl power," and more optimistic than their parents. These egalitarian, communitarian impulses lead them to volunteer in record numbers—tutoring underprivileged children, cleaning up state parks, building homes for the homeless, and feeding those without food. They are staying away from the voting booth, but not from community life. In fact, a growing number of young people believe that volunteering is more important than voting, a message continually reinforced by a culture that lavishly praises community service and too often treats politics as if it is a communicable disease.

So the apathy and disengagement that young people exhibit toward the political process can't simply be dismissed as another example of what Thomas Patterson, Bradlee Professor of Government and the Press at Harvard University, calls "the vanishing voter." Instead of merely opting out, they are creating their own political and civic culture, rewriting the rules of citizenship, in ways both inspiring and dangerous to democracy. The inspiration comes from the selflessness of it all—the way high school kids will spend their summer building a school lunchroom in an impoverished community and college grads will forgo a comfortable salary to teach the students no one else will teach.

"Community service is the new politics," says Ganesh Sitaraman, who coauthored *Invisible Citizens: Youth Politics After September 11* while a student at Harvard University. "The thing to be involved with in the Sixties was political protests. That's now being completely replaced by community service. Even schools are promoting the idea of service instead of politics as an alternative way of creating change."

But this alternative could have grave consequences for the health of our government and the future of American political life. Helping poor kids to read in a volunteer after-school program is not going to get them the new building they badly need. That is still government's job. Clearing paths in an overgrown state park cannot replace the need for broader conservation measures to preserve our natural resources and environment, which only the public sector can implement and monitor. Young people can work weekends with local congregations to rehabilitate abandoned houses, but that won't make more than a tiny dent in homelessness or significantly increase the supply of affordable housing for low-income families. As Ira Harkavy, director of the Center for Community Partnerships at the University of Pennsylvania, said at a forum on national service in 2002: "It's not enough to serve soup in a soup kitchen. We have to work toward ending the conditions that make people hungry."

Not all of those conditions are caused by government policy, nor do all of the answers come from City Hall or Capitol Hill. Creative partnerships with private, religious, and community organizations are key to building what Robert Putnam, professor of public policy at Harvard University, calls the "social capital" necessary to address the issues facing twenty-first-century American life. Yet, as he wrote in his latest book, *Better Together*, "The argument sometimes heard that civil society alone can solve public issues if only the state would get out of the way is simply silly."

Local, state, and national governments will always be the irreplaceable linchpins in setting communal agendas and guarding the common good. In a representative democracy, choosing who serves in those governments and holding them accountable every Election Day is the central role of a citizen. The strength of a government and its capacity to exert power and moral authority rests on the degree of support it has from the electorate. As Abbie Hoffman once said back in the sixties,

"Democracy is not something you believe in or a place to hang your hat. You participate. If you stop doing it, democracy crumbles."

If young people continue to stay home on Election Day and direct their considerable energies toward fixing a piece of the problem rather than the whole, it follows that citizenship will essentially become privatized, a province of the involved few who will look after their own rights and concerns, and care about the common good only when it suits them. Already we are witnessing what Michael Schudson, professor of communications at the University of California, San Diego, calls the evolution of the "rights-bearing citizen," ready to defend his or her rights in the courtroom or the voting booth. That can be an empowering development, but consider what would happen if it was taken to the extreme: a representative democracy driven solely by those clever (or wealthy) enough to protect themselves. We do not want our elected officials answerable only to the few. Young people should not be left out of the process simply because it requires too much effort to bring them in.

It must be said at the outset that this is not just a problem plaguing America but a feature of contemporary life in most of the world's democracies. According to a major study by the International Institute for Democracy and Electoral Assistance (IDEA), voter turnout across the globe rose steadily from 1945 to 1990 and has declined since, especially among the young. In the parliamentary democracies in Western Europe, with the exceptions of Belgium and Italy, voter turnout by young people is substantially lower than for the population as a whole; in some nations, the gap is larger than 20 percent. There, too, the trend defies tradition, since the young have a markedly higher level of education than their elders, and therefore should be more inclined to vote.

Once again, the United States is leading a civic trend,

though in this case it's a dubious distinction. For while youth voting rates are declining in other democracies, their descent started decades after ours and from a higher base. Despite the gloomy assessment in the IDEA report, youth turnout among the fifteen nations studied still averaged over 80 percent.

We can only wish for that number in America. Or we can commit ourselves to take the necessary steps, modest and sweeping, to reverse the trend and lead democracy again in a new, robust direction.

On that Tuesday morning thirty-five years ago in Washington, when the last chapter in the long quest for universal suffrage was being written, Sen. Jacob K. Javits, a New York Republican, rose to offer some historical context of his own.

"Mr. Chairman," he said, "it has always been difficult to enlarge the voting franchise in this country. The colonists who wanted to remove ownership of property as a requirement for voting faced similar arguments about a deluge of irresponsible people entering the voting roles. So did those who fought to grant the vote to women, and those who joined in the struggle to assure the vote to Negroes. But in each case, the eventual expansion of the electorate brought new ideas and new vigor to our national political life. So it is here."

It is not too late to see that promise fulfilled.

CHAPTER TWO

Jennings Randolph's Obsession:
Why one man worked for nearly thirty years to secure the right to vote for eighteen-year-olds

When Idell Bingham Randolph gave birth to a son on March 8, 1902, in Salem, West Virginia, she and her husband, Ernest, named their child Jennings, after the great orator and statesman William Jennings Bryan, whose repeated, quixotic runs for president, principled stands on foreign policy, and tireless campaigns for workers' rights and women's suffrage had captured the hearts of many in hardscrabble Appalachia.

As luck would have it, when Jennings Randolph took a seat in the U.S. House of Representatives in 1933, he was given an introductory tour of Capitol Hill by none other than Ruth Bryan Owen, at the time a Democratic congresswoman from Florida and the daughter of the man whose name Randolph was given. The new congressman was determined to pick up his hero's banner. A self-described "Jeffersonian Democrat," he was a staunch supporter of the New Deal in the 1930s, was instrumental in building the interstate highway system in the 1940s, and steered countless federal dollars to struggling Appalachian communities back home. In later years he threw his considerable political clout behind the Civil Rights Act and Lyndon B. Johnson's anti-poverty programs. He earned the unending fealty of the nation's blind by championing their right to open up newspaper vending stands in federal office buildings.

But in addition to all those accomplishments, he worked for nearly thirty years in the U.S. Congress, first in the House and then in the Senate, to lower the legal voting age from twenty-one to eighteen. His obsession began shortly after he cast the decisive vote approving President Roosevelt's war preparations draft in 1940, when he concluded that the young people he had just helped draft to fight in Europe and the Far East ought to be able to vote if they returned home alive.

In late 1942, he drafted and introduced legislation to enfranchise eighteen-, nineteen-, and twenty-year-olds. The measure went nowhere. Undeterred, he introduced the legislation again, and again. All told, it took ten more attempts before the bill was finally enacted, and Jennings Randolph would watch with satisfaction as the Twenty-sixth Amendment became law on June 30, 1971. "I believe that our young people possess a great social conscience, are perplexed by the injustices which exist in the world, and are anxious to rectify those ills," Randolph said as his long-sought dream became the law of the land.

The story of the Twenty-sixth Amendment is important for several reasons. It reflects the history of suffrage in America, a complicated narrative of rights given and then sometimes taken away, as those rights were for blacks in the South. But the story is also about the courage to grow the democratic experience; it has always depended on the prescient beliefs of a few farsighted individuals stubborn enough to ride into uncharted territory to reach a destination that seems inevitable only in retrospect. It took decades—centuries, really—for the vote to be given to eighteen-year-olds, but when it finally happened, the Twenty-sixth Amendment to the Constitution was ratified more quickly than any in the history of the Republic. As we struggle today with the decline in youth voting and all that portends, history can be a guide and an inspiration.

"It is by no means self-evident, as one looks at modern history, that individuals who possess political power will (or can be expected to) share that power with others, millions of others," writes Alexander Keyssar in the introduction to his excellent survey book, *The Right to Vote: The Contested History of Democracy in the United States.* "This history of suffrage in the United States is a history of both expansion and contraction, of inclusion and exclusion, of shifts in direction and momentum at different places and at different times."

In fact, the first serious consideration of lowering the voting age to eighteen did not come in our own time, but a century earlier. On June 19, 1867, a delegate to the Constitutional Convention of the State of New York by the name of Marcus Bickford proposed that the convention "inquire into and report on the expediency and propriety of extending the elective franchise to native-born male citizens of this State, between the ages of eighteen and twenty-one."

His reasoning foreshadowed an argument that would be made repeatedly for the next one hundred years, though he made it in nineteenth-century terms: "Before the flood, when man lived to the age of nearly a thousand years, a child of a hundred was still a child. . . ." Bickford told the convention. "Afterward we find Isaac emancipating his sons Esau and Jacob at the age of forty. Under the Jewish economy the age of majority was fixed at twenty-five. Now, sir, the age in which we live, in this fast age, men arrive to maturity both in body and mind at a great deal earlier period than formerly."

This was surely an argument made before its time. Bickford's amendment was defeated by a vote of 82 to 33. No one else took up the cause. Twenty-one was to remain the official age of majority.

* * *

Not until the Second World War did the subject come up again with any seriousness. In 1941, a year before President Franklin Delano Roosevelt signed legislation lowering the draft age to eighteen and even before the bombing of Pearl Harbor, Senator Harley Kilgore, a West Virginia Democrat, offered a voting age amendment, but it went nowhere. Then in October 1942, days after the draft was enacted, Senator Arthur Vandenberg, a Michigan Republican, and U.S. Representative Jennings Randolph, another West Virginia Democrat, introduced identical resolutions. They also went nowhere.

Exactly why Jennings Randolph took up the cause again when the new congressional session opened in January 1943 is something of a mystery. Perhaps it was because Senator Kilgore was also from West Virginia. Perhaps it was because Randolph had cast the deciding vote approving Roosevelt's war preparations draft, and now wanted to make sure that new soldiers could become full new citizens.

Jay Randolph thinks this passion for suffrage was in his father's blood. Now a well-known sports broadcaster living in St. Louis, Missouri, the younger Randolph said he heard his father talk incessantly about the importance of the vote "from the time I was old enough to know what's going on." Just as Salem, West Virginia, was the family town—ancestor Samuel Fitz Randolph received the deed for the land in the 1780s—politics was the family avocation. Ernest Randolph was a petroleum producer, attorney, and cattle shipper in Salem, but what Jay remembers especially about his grandfather was that he ran for the U.S. Congress and lost. Clearly, his only son, Jennings, was raised to take up the mantle of politics, and perhaps the cause of suffrage as well.

At Salem College, a Seventh Day Baptist institution founded by his grandfather and now known as Salem International University, Jennings Randolph was active in campus politics and sports, "a kind of political animal and talented public speaker," Jay Randolph recalls. After graduating in 1924, Jennings Randolph worked as a newspaper reporter, editor, and college professor before launching his own attempt to gain a congressional seat. His first run in 1930 was unsuccessful; two years later, propelled by the Roosevelt landslide and his well-known oratory, he won as a populist Democrat from a populist Democratic state.

Campaigning in those days in a place like West Virginia was like selling a product door-to-door. From morning until night, Randolph would stop at every little store, coal mine, and front stoop, and with his gift for public oratory, his fetching optimism and down-home demeanor persuade his listeners to vote. To vote for him, of course, but also to vote.

Jay Randolph recalls that his father carried with him a list of famous votes, in Congress and from around the world, that were decided by one person, as if to underscore the importance of a single act and the power of a single individual. "It was a real crusade for him," the son says. "He was an extremely optimistic man and had a great drive in regard to the democratic process."

* * *

It took a while for the democratic process—and popular opinion—to catch up with Jennings Randolph. Momentum began to build slowly in 1943, when First Lady Eleanor Roosevelt endorsed the eighteen-year-old vote, and the National Education Association threw in its support. Four other Congressmen introduced their own resolutions. The state of Georgia became, in August of that year, the first state to amend its constitution to extend the franchise downward. A bitter gubernatorial campaign left young voters particularly emboldened and angry, so they pushed the amendment through in what even supporters say was a surprising state to lead the charge of liberalizing suffrage.

As Governor Ellis Arnall said at the time: "If there had ever been a State in the Union where I, offhand, would have believed the people would have been slow to reduce the voting age, I would have picked my own, the State of Georgia." When asked why, he replied: "Because we have such conservative people, and yet they ratified this amendment." By a 2:1 vote, one might add. (Interestingly, the new "teen-age voters," as they were called, were exempt from paying the poll tax until they were 21.)

Governor Arnall was the star witness on October 20, 1943, at the first and only hearing held by a subcommittee of the House Judiciary Committee on Randolph's proposed amendment. (None of the other resolutions ever made it to the hearing stage.) Randolph surely needed Arnall; Georgia stood then as the lonely anomaly among states, since thirty others had rejected similar moves in the last year. Randolph appeared undeterred: "I can well understand, Mr. Chairman, that originally a proposition of this kind will receive opposition. That was true of the amendment that gave the voting rights to women. I can remember, as a young man, listening to heated debate in my State on the subject of woman suffrage."

His argument then remained his argument for decades, a forceful entreaty for fairness combined with a stalwart idealism. Fairness concerned the millions of young people who were fighting in Europe, Africa, and Southeast Asia but could not vote back home: 25 percent of those serving in the army were between eighteen and twenty years old; 37 percent of the navy; 50 percent of the marines. Each, Randolph knew, had a story. "Private John McEachern, of Roxbury Crossing, Massachusetts, went into the army at eighteen. As a paratrooper at nineteen years of age, he lost his life in North Africa fighting," Randolph told his colleagues. "Private Everett Sparks, of Marietta, Ohio, left his home and parents at twenty, and today lies buried somewhere amidst the cruel and drifting mists of Kiska, or on the agonizing fogbound island of Attu. Who shall say: They were not old enough to have been voting citizens of the America for which they gave their lives?"

Governor Arnall offered the idealistic argument, as he cited the improvements in education, civic knowledge, and overall maturity that he believed characterized the next generation. "It amuses me," Arnall told the hearing, "when some people say young people are addicted to taking up foreign subversive ideas. As far as I am concerned, I have never seen an eighteen-year-old American boy who did not believe that someday he was going to own his business, someday he was going to be a millionaire, and someday he was going to be President of the United States. I believe in American youth. If you allow the people, through their State legislatures, to put into effect a system that will permit youth voting in this Nation, you will bring to our electorate a high degree of intelligence and courage and candor and enthusiasm badly needed today.... And I want to tell you gentlemen of this subcommittee that any nation that is distrustful of its youth is headed for destruction and ruin."

Of course, Arnall also had a story to tell. To wit:

A young man came to see me who had been at Guadalcanal. For nine months he was at an outpost in jungle land, separated from his comrades.

I said, "What did you think about when you were out there?"

He said, "I had reconciled myself to the fact I was going to be killed. I thought about my life and what I had done. I thought about my family, my mother and my father. And I thought about my sweetheart. I thought about my country, for which I was going to die. And I thought about God."

Can anyone stand up and tell me that such a young patriot is not entitled to the simple right to register his feeling about government policies? I say it is not fair and it is not right.

You would think such arguments would win the day, or at least attract a few new supporters. But at 3:10 that afternoon, after slightly more than an hour, the subcommittee adjourned without voting, and without indicating when next it would bring up Jennings Randolph's legislation. If ever.

* * *

While Congress would hem and haw for another generation, the debate over the legal voting age had clearly piqued the nation's interest. The *Congressional Digest* issued a hefty special volume in August–September 1944 on the subject, publishing page upon page of arguments, pro and con. "What effect the end of the war will have on a question born of war, remains to be seen," the *Digest* opined in its introduction.

Jennings Randolph was given top billing, and he mustered his usual eloquence to argue for the fairness and the benefit of bringing young people into the voting process. It appears that such an argument was getting harder to publicly rebuke. Or so wrote U.S. Representative Emanuel Celler, the powerful New York Democrat, who complained that it "is apparently just as difficult to oppose a teen-age voting right as it would be to oppose free lunches or a soldier's bonus or 'equal right.' Sentimental issues," Celler cried, "have, somehow, managed to get entangled with the fundamentals of democracy."

He held up his side of the debate forcefully. Joining the armed forces is not connected to the right to vote, he wrote. The age of twenty-one has always been the age of majority in the United States, and those nations that do allow eighteen-year-olds to vote—such as Germany, Italy, Russia, and Spain—are "the least liberty-loving." Young men, Celler further argued, are easily persuaded and emotional, prone to grasp at panaceas, without the judgment necessary for true citizenship and are often illiterate and ill informed. "Before we expand the number of voters," he concluded, "let us first spend our energies in increasing wisdom of those who now vote and in improving the mean intelligence of the nation."

As a testament to their political skill and longevity, both Randolph and Celler were still in Congress when the resolution that would become the Twenty-sixth Amendment was finally approved twenty-seven years later. Sometime after he penned those arguments in opposition, though, Emanuel Celler had a change of heart and mind. Only nineteen members of Congress voted "no" in 1971, and he was not among them.

History affords us a glance backwards that so often makes the uncertain seem inevitable. But we do the debate of 1944 a disservice if we don't see that those opposed to the eighteen-year-old vote were prescient, too. The last page of the *Congressional Digest* special issue contained pro and con statements from two recent high school graduates. James F. Concannon from William Howard Taft High School in Chicago succinctly argued that his generation was mature, educated, and devoted enough to deserve the right to vote. John E. Walker, of the Ocala High School in Ocala, Florida, begged to differ. When he was eighteen, Walker noted, he had neither the interest nor the capacity to reach the considered opinion necessary for an informed vote.

"But," he added, "let us suppose you did give the eighteen-to twenty-year-old group the vote during the war. Remember, that even if they have a zeal for public affairs now, this will diminish considerably once the war is over.... I believe that after the war the lower-age group would be inclined to become indifferent to politics. The younger the voter, the less likely he is to exercise his voting privilege. To force suffrage upon a group which would probably be indifferent would be not only unsuccessful but downright disastrous."

How could he have known?

* * *

Jennings Randolph lost his seat in Congress in the Republican sweep of 1946. He stayed on in Washington, working for the aviation industry and in college administration, while keeping his hand in West Virginia politics by serving as a delegate to the Democratic national conventions in 1948, 1952, and 1956.

Meantime, the movement to reduce the voting age hobbled

along as it tried to persuade state lawmakers to change their constitutions. Proponents of women's suffrage could have told them that was a slow and often fruitless strategy, and "the youth vote movement, moreover, was inescapably weakened by the fact that its membership was inherently transitory," as Alexander Keyssar notes in *The Right to Vote*. Any eighteen-year-old can simply wait a few years and he'll be eligible to vote.

Yet popular opinion was slowly moving in favor of extending the franchise, helped along, no doubt, by the exigencies of the Korean War and President Eisenhower's vocal support for a constitutional amendment in 1952. A Gallup poll released in July 1953 showed that 60 percent of American college students favored a voting age of eighteen, and only 38 percent were opposed. Support was almost as strong in polls surveying the population as a whole.

Responding to the president's plea, Senate Judiciary Committee chairman William Langer, a North Dakota Republican, even held hearings on his own legislation. The resolution was actually brought to the floor of the Senate on May 21, 1954, for a vote, but a coalition of liberal Democrats and moderate Republicans was unable to obtain the required two-thirds majority for passage. After a full day's debate, there were 34 yeas, 24 nays, and a total of 37 senators who, in an act of legislative bravery, did not vote at all. Southern Democrats, it seemed, were particularly loath to surrender what they saw as the states' right to establish the rules of the franchise.

Fortunately for the youth vote movement, Jennings Randolph was headed back to Capitol Hill. Elected in 1958 to fill out the balance of a deceased senator's term, Randolph joined seventeen other Senate newcomers who were generally more liberal than their predecessors. With names like Edmund S. Muskie of Maine, Eugene J. McCarthy of Minnesota, Thomas J. Dodd of Connecticut, and Randolph's longtime friend and

Senate partner, Robert C. Byrd of West Virginia, it was possible to see where the movement was headed.

And then came the 1960s and the election of the youthful president John F. Kennedy. The legislation he sent to Congress to enfranchise the residents of the District of Columbia called on the vote to be extended to eighteen-year-olds, but that was beaten back by Republicans in committee. Still, a slew of bills were introduced to reduce the voting age, although it's necessary to point out that a paucity of legislation was never the movement's problem. As Wendell W. Cultice points out in his book, *Youth's Battle for the Ballot,* from 1925 to 1964, nearly five-dozen proposals had been introduced on behalf of youth suffrage.

A presidential commission charged with investigating the causes of the widespread failure to register and vote—which seem quaint compared to the failures of today—was appointed by President Kennedy before his death and reported to the new President Johnson in late 1963. Among other things, it recommended that states "should carefully consider reducing the minimum voting age to 18" and promote the vote in high school citizenship programs. "Why should it be so difficult for people to vote?" asked President Johnson when he officially received the report. "It is easier now to register and enlist in the service in many cases than it is to vote. Why should a man have an easy path provided for him to go and fight, but a difficult path for him to go and vote?"

Good question. It was, unfortunately, difficult for Johnson to answer as he became more embroiled in the miasma of Vietnam, and as opposition to the war grew louder and stronger, underscoring the lack of enfranchisement of the very people most affected by the prolonged military conflict. Numerous states began considering legislation to lower the voting age, and support was growing in all corners of the political spectrum,

from conservative Republicans to antiwar Democrats, but-
tressed by unions, church associations, student groups, civic
organizations, and lobbying coalitions. Three months after his
dramatic decision not to seek reelection, President Johnson
in June 1967 officially proposed that the U.S. Constitution be
amended to enfranchise eighteen-year-olds. A cartoon from
the *Buffalo Evening News* shows a soldier in Vietnam holding a
newspaper with word of LBJ's announcement: "They're gonna
treat me like a man," he cries.

As Fred P. Graham wrote in the *New York Times*: "The proposal to lower the voting age to 18 years, a perennial loser in
Congress in recent decades, has taken on new life following recent campus revolts."

The first major round of hearings was convened by Senator
Birch Bayh, the Indiana Democrat who chaired the subcommittee of the Senate's Judiciary Committee, on May 14, 1968. A
staunch proponent of expanding the franchise, Bayh had tried
unsuccessfully to persuade the Indiana legislature to lower the
voting age back when he was a state lawmaker in the 1950s. Now
presiding over a key committee in Congress, he was duty bound
to hear dissenters, and there were plenty of them. The raucous
protests roiling college campuses and public spaces were reason
for Bayh to believe that young people deserve the vote; they
were reason for others to reject it. "[M]any teenagers, lacking
the experience and maturity, are prone to take an extreme point
of view and to push their ideas to the exclusion of all others,"
maintained Senator Jack Miller, an Iowa Republican. "One
need only look at what has happened and is happening on the
campuses of some of our great universities to see the results of
this lack of maturity."

And the following day, Senator Spessard L. Holland, Democrat of Florida, continued the thought, or rather the warning.
"Mr. Chairman," he said sternly, "one reason in particular that

should make us want to move slowly in lowering age requirements for voting is the thought of political organizations moving into our college campuses, which they would do with a
vengeance if the students were voters. This would be a most
dangerous situation since the years eighteen to twenty-one are
now, as they have been in previous years, formative years where
youth is reaching maturity during which time his attitude shifts
from place to place, and are the years of great uncertainties,
which are a fertile ground for demagogues, for youth attaches
itself to promises rather than to performance."

That view was repudiated kindly but forcefully the next day,
as the floor was graciously given to Senator Randolph, whom
Bayh called "almost a founding father of this movement." Not-
ing that he introduced the first resolution back in 1942, Randolph said, "My interest in this subject has not abated. I had
then, as I have now, the utmost confidence in the ability of our
young citizens to think clearly, to weigh the issues, and to make
judicious decisions on matters closely affecting their futures."

It is fascinating to read such starkly different assessments of
a single generation. But the debate over suffrage in America has
always been about more than just the minutiae of electoral process. At its core, it is a debate about identity and the value placed
on groups of citizens and their worthiness to participate in the
whole of American life. Blacks were denied the vote because
they were denied the dignity of being a whole person. Women
were kept away from balloting because men did not think they
were worthy of the task. These groups were different, unpredictable. And so it was with youth. When Randolph said later at
that hearing, "I am not worried when people differ, Mr. Chairman. Differences do not alarm me. It is only when people are
indifferent that I have great concern"—you hear no fear in his
voice, only the optimistic belief that the opportunity to participate turns even the protestor and the dissenter into a citizen.

As Birch Bayh later said of Randolph, "I just think he was a true believer."

Today, we occasionally hear the words of a true believer, or at least an election-night convert—those who thank the wisdom of the populace if it helped them win and greet it with a polite shrug otherwise. But the stirring, enunciated belief that the inclusion of young people into the political process would benefit the nation barely gets a mention in public discourse. That's part of the problem. We don't say it because we don't believe it, and young people hear *that* message loud and clear.

* * *

On August 12, 1969, Jennings Randolph once again introduced a joint resolution proposing an amendment to the Constitution to lower the voting age, only this time he was joined by sixty-seven co-sponsors. In another round of hearings in February and March of the next year, broad support for the amendment was expressed—but sometimes with qualification. Testifying for the Nixon administration, Deputy Attorney General Richard Kleindienst said that America's 10 million young people between the ages of eighteen and twenty-one deserved the right to vote not because they were old enough to fight, but because they were smart enough to vote. "Their well-informed intelligence, enthusiastic interest, and desire to participate in public affairs at all levels exemplifies the highest qualities of mature citizenship," he said in a prepared statement. And so Richard Nixon became the third U.S. president to propose a constitutional amendment to enfranchise eighteen-year-olds. But in a nod to the states' rights mind-set in the South, he thought that the amendment should apply only to those voting for federal offices—president, vice president, and members of Congress. States should have the right to set eligibility standards for their elections, he argued.

Although Bayh was reported at the time to support the proposed compromise as "half a loaf rather than no loaf at all," it was roundly criticized by others who testified at the hearings that winter. Former attorney general Ramsey Clark said that such "halfway steps are one of the causes" of young people's belief that the system cannot act swiftly or meaningfully. "We subject ten to twelve million young citizens between seventeen and twenty-one years of age to taxation without representation. This is four times the population of the Colonies the night the tea was dumped in Boston Harbor."

Nonetheless, compromise was in the air.

Mike Mansfield, the Senate majority leader from Montana, and his colleague, a very young Edward Kennedy, Democrat of Massachusetts, hatched a plot that was shaky on constitutional grounds but brilliant politically. On March 4, 1970, Mansfield offered an amendment to the extension of the Voting Rights Act that would lower the voting age to eighteen in all federal, state, and local elections. This wasn't the laborious constitutional route that Jennings Randolph had advocated for many years. This was, Mansfield and Kennedy argued, a shorter path to enfranchisement.

Kennedy believed that he had the scholars to prove it—two eminent constitutional authorities who unequivocally stated that Congress had the power under the Constitution to reduce the voting age by statute, without having to go through all the trouble of passing a constitutional amendment and then waiting until two-thirds of the states ratified it. The scholars argued that Congress, in implementing the equal protection clause of the Fourteenth Amendment, had the power to decide whether the states were imposing an unreasonable qualification for voting. Denying the vote to eighteen-year-olds, it followed, was unreasonable.

This line of thinking astonished other constitutional schol-

ars and infuriated some senators, but Mansfield was nothing if
not a clever politician. Since the extension of the Voting Rights
Act and its protections against racial discrimination hung in the
balance, this was a pretty hard measure to oppose. The Senate
approved it by a wide, bipartisan margin of 64 to 17 (with 14
abstentions).

The House was a different story. On lowering the voting age,
the House was always a different story, thanks to the stubborn
opposition of Emanuel Celler, the eighty-one-year-old New
York Democrat who went up against Jennings Randolph on this
issue twenty-five years earlier. Celler, the powerful chair of the
House Judiciary Committee, promised to "fight like hell" to kill
the provision. He was determined to take the legislation to the
Senate-House conference, where he would insist on stripping
the voting age amendment from the voting rights extension.

Speaker of the House John W. McCormack thought otherwise. The seventy-eight-year-old political elder had already
announced his retirement and decided to make a push for the
lowered voting age his last legislative hurrah. Given five minutes
of precious debate time to state his views, the craggy, white-
haired McCormack rose to the floor on June 16, 1970, and reminded his colleagues that if the resolution went to conference,
the Voting Rights Act extension would be endangered and the
cause of eighteen-year-old voting might be delayed a decade,
or even two. Then he concluded, almost regally, "In the closing
seconds of the time allotted to me—and I shall not be back here
next year—might I make a personal observation. Nothing
would make John McCormack happier than to see this resolution adopted."

The final vote was even larger than some supporters had
expected—272 to 132. The galleries, packed with an unusually
large number of young people, burst into applause. "One of the
unending debates in Congress is whether a given moment

qualifies as historic, but in a House of many lows and lulls, this moment certainly approached such distinction," Wendell Cultice noted in his exhaustive history of that debate. "In little more than an hour on that day, the House extended the privilege to vote to 11 million young Americans and preserved one of the nation's most significant civil rights programs."

It was too soon, however, to break out the champagne.

* * *

The vote was seen as an enormous victory for those who engineered the successful parliamentary maneuver. But even a supporter like Birch Bayh acknowledged to me in a 2003 interview that, no matter what a few scholars said, "there were significant questions about its constitutionality." So significant that President Nixon's deep ambivalence was underscored in two ways. First, while signing House Resolution 4249, he directed the attorney general to seek a swift court test of its constitutionality and, at the same time, urged Congress to hurry up with legislation to lower the voting age by constitutional amendment instead of by legislative fiat.

The second way in which the president's ambivalence was evident was noted by Wendell Cultice: "Nixon signed the bill in his hideaway office shortly after lunch with only an aide for an audience and with his own silver fountain pen, foreswearing the ceremonial signing and distribution of souvenir pens often associated with historic bill signings."

That would come much later.

The legal challenges came immediately.

* * *

What followed was, essentially, a quiet confusion that slowly built into political chaos. Those 11 million potential new voters were not yet entitled to participate in the November 1970 elections. In the meantime, the Nixon administration ordered states to prepare for eighteen-year-old voters, but many did not. Sooner or later, the U.S. Supreme Court was going to have to resolve this issue. Fortunately for the nation, it was sooner.

After the confusing summer of 1970, the high court agreed to hear a challenge to the new law on October 19, when four lawsuits were consolidated into what became known as *Oregon v. Mitchell*. The oral arguments that had been rehearsed for decades were repeated again, this time with a heightened sense of urgency. After all, a presidential election was on the horizon, and in most states it was not at all clear who could vote for what.

When the Supreme Court issued what became known as the "Christmas Decision," coming as it did on December 21, the landscape became even stranger; the confusion turned into chaos. This was one of the most unusual rulings in the history of the Republic.

Four justices—William J. Brennan Jr., William O. Douglas, Thurgood Marshall, and Byron R. White—believed that the congressional action to enfranchise eighteen-year-olds was entirely constitutional and argued that the law should stand. Four other justices—Harry A. Blackmun, John M. Harlan, Potter Stewart, and the chief justice, Warren Burger—argued that the law was unconstitutional in all state and federal elections and should be struck down. An even tie.

So what became the majority opinion was written by the ninth justice, eighty-four-year-old Hugo L. Black, even though none of the other justices actually agreed with him. Black believed that the 1970 congressional action was constitutional when it came to election to federal office and ordered states to allow citizens between eighteen and twenty-one years old to vote in federal elections. But he also argued that states retained the power to set the minimum age in state and local elections, and therefore left it up to the lawmakers in fifty states to enlarge the franchise, or not.

In his opinion, Black argued that the Constitution clearly gives Congress the right to set the voting qualifications for congressional and presidential elections. "A newly created national government could hardly have been expected to survive without the ultimate power to rule itself and fill its offices under its own laws," he wrote. But, he added, "the Constitution was also intended to preserve to the States the power that even the Colonies had to establish and maintain their own separate and independent governments."

It's hard to underestimate the confusion this ruling created. At the time of the court's decision, eighteen-year-olds could vote in only three states: Alaska, Georgia, and Kentucky. Nineteen-year-olds could vote in three other states: Montana, Minnesota, and Massachusetts. Twenty-year-olds could cast a ballot in still three other states: Hawaii, Maine, and Nebraska. Americans in the forty-one remaining states had to wait until they were twenty-one to enter the voting booth. Even if lawmakers wanted to rush out on December 22 and amend their state constitutions to meet the new federal minimum age, many could not complete the work before the 1972 presidential election.

Now this patchwork system was going to be stretched perhaps beyond the breaking point. The laws of most states lagged far behind overall public opinion, in which a growing and comfortable majority favored lowering the voting age. Nonetheless, most states were now faced with the unenviable task of figuring out which of their citizens could register and subsequently vote for president, but not for governor or state legislator or, for that matter, dogcatcher if that office was still subject to local balloting. This was an administrative nightmare and, to some degree, a moral failure on the part of the nation's leaders to establish clear, sensible, and enforceable standards for voting.

A Senate report, issued in February 1971 by Senator Birch Bayh's subcommittee on constitutional amendments, called the decision "morally indefensible." The report also complained that separate voting arrangements would be needed for more than 10 million voters in the 1972 presidential election if the dual-age voting system prevailed. A memorandum prepared for the secretary of state of Minnesota predicted "a nightmare at best." And an expensive one. The cost of administering separate registration facilities, purchasing new voting machines, hiring extra personnel, printing two sets of ballots, etc., would amount to at least $10 to $20 million a year, said the report.

It got worse. In addition to cost and general confusion, there also was the dilemma of determining just what a federal election is. An arcane matter, perhaps, but in some states a crucial one. For in some states, the selection of nominees for federal offices is performed by elected delegates who are also chosen to perform state election tasks. Delegates to the Indiana state party conventions (Bayh's home state) in turn select delegates to their party's national convention, so that would clearly be included in an eighteen-year-old's ballot. But those delegates also chose the party's candidate for governor. Would the eighteen-year-old still be allowed to vote for them?

I asked Bayh whether this maneuver by Congress to initially bypass amending the Constitution made any sense in retrospect, especially since it caused so much confusion and uncertainty. He takes the legislator's view of history—that is, the long view.

"It was worth a try," he still believes. "It was easier to get a majority vote than the two-thirds needed for the constitutional amendment. Once we were successful in that bifurcated court decision, it made it impossible for legislatures to deny the right to vote (for eighteen-year-olds) on the state level. There are no absolutes in Congress," he reminded me. "Often goals are achieved by increments. I'd like to see justice immediately prevail in the legislative process, but sometimes you have to wait."

* * *

Fortunately for the eighteen-year-olds of America, the wait was not too long. As Alexander Keyssar noted in his history of suffrage: "Faced with this crisis, Congress moved expeditiously to rectify the mess that it had helped to create."

Once again, now for the eleventh time in his life, Jennings Randolph introduced a proposed constitutional amendment, Senate Joint Resolution 7, on January 25, 1971; it had eighty-six co-sponsors. It was referred to Bayh's committee, then to the full Senate Judiciary Committee, which reported it out favorably to the Senate on March 8. Two days later, the full Senate approved the resolution to amend the constitution: 94 yeas—not a single objection.

The companion resolution in the House was introduced by none other than Representative Emmanuel Celler, the staunch opponent who now raised his powerful banner in favor of the youth vote. It was approved on March 23 by a vote of 400 to 19. The House then endorsed the Senate version and effectively put aside its own. Jennings Randolph finally was able to witness his beloved United States Congress overwhelmingly approve the cause to which he had dedicated nearly three decades of hard, sometimes lonely, work.

States now scrambled to approve the proposed Twenty-sixth Amendment to the Constitution. Five states—Connecticut, Delaware, Minnesota, Tennessee, and Washington—did so on March 23, the very day it became law on Capitol Hill. Wendell Cultice called it a "blitzkrieg ratification," the swiftest ever in American history.

In the end, the race to clamber aboard this bandwagon was almost comical. The ratification of at least thirty-eight states, or three-fourths of the total, is required for constitutional amendments, and by spring of 1971, the list was growing rapidly. New York ratified on June 2, then Oregon, Missouri, Wisconsin, Illinois, and finally Alabama, after a filibuster by a central Alabama conservative lawmaker ended when he (literally) took his seat, exhausted. North Carolina's ratification also was held up by internal opposition, but it eventually became the thirty-seventh state. Ohio was in line to be number 38, a position its state officials inexplicably craved, surprising especially since only two years earlier an attempt to lower the voting age statewide was killed by a margin of 45,000 votes.

Not willing to put this before the voters again, lawmakers decided to ratify the amendment through the legislature. The stage was set. On June 29, the Ohio state senate approved the measure by a vote of 30 to 2. The next day it was the House's turn. The Republican speaker of the House, Charles F. Kurfess, had planned to let a number of members of both parties speak on the issue before a vote was called. But, as R. W. Apple Jr. reported in the *New York Times,* an "atmosphere of near-panic attended Ohio's climactic vote."

After three short speeches, the GOP floor leader interrupted to warn: "I've just been informed that the legislature of Oklahoma has gone into special session tonight. The time for debate and discussion is over. The time for action is here."

Then, as the *Columbus Evening Dispatch* reported the next day, Kurfess, "liberally exercising his gavel and ignoring the outraged screams of opponents, pushed the ratification resolution through the House in 12 minutes, picking up his pen to sign the measure at 8:02 P.M." One lawmaker yelled, "What ever happened to free speech?" The question left unanswered, the heavy-handed tactics worked, and the measure was handily approved, 81 to 9.

Ohio's place of distinction was secure.

The official certification of the Twenty-sixth Amendment came a few days later, on Monday, July 5. This time, President Nixon didn't hide in a White House office, furtively signing a bill he probably wished would go away. This time, more than five hundred members of a singing group called Young Americans in Concert witnessed the event in the East Room of the White House, as the president bent over a mahogany desk thought to have been used by Thomas Jefferson during the Continental Congress centuries ago in Philadelphia. This time, pens were kept as souvenirs by the three eighteen-year-old witnesses dressed in blue blazers and starched white blouses.

"The country needs an infusion of new spirit from time to time," Nixon told the assembled group. "As I stand here, I sense that we can have confidence that America's new votes will provide what this country needs."

One chapter of American history closed, and another one opened, uncertainly.

* * *

What happens when all that work and struggle is greeted by a collective yawn? In the years before he died in 1998, Jennings Randolph agonized over the growing apathy and cynicism of young people, frequently exhorting them to exercise the "franchise of freedom," as he called it. "In his later years," Jay Randolph remembered of his father, "he was so proud and yet so disappointed that young people weren't going to the polls."

Do we vote now only because it was once unattainable for so many? No. But history does bear down on each of us when we step into that booth and draw the curtain; we can't shape the future without some idea of what made the past. The story of suffrage in America is a tale of rights given, and rights taken away. Thanks to Jennings Randolph and scores of other lawmakers, lobbyists, and loyal democrats, any law-abiding citizen gets to vote by virtue of reaching the age of eighteen. But that right was granted with the explicit expectation that young people would serve the nation and contribute to its betterment. It wasn't won easily, and it didn't come free.

CHAPTER THREE

"An Unexpected Coming of Age": Why so many young Americans voted in 1972, even when the outcome of the election was never in doubt

My students in PSCI-298 at the University of Pennsylvania in the fall of 2003 were given this assignment on the first day of class: Find someone who voted for the first time in 1972. Ask them what it was like, what it meant. And be prepared to share what you've learned in class the next week.

I confess, this was a selfish assignment on my part. I asked them to collect the stories because, as someone a year too young to vote in that momentous election, I wanted to hear what it was like for those just ahead of me in line. I continually felt like the little sister in those days, denied protest marches and Woodstock and so many other cool things because I was a smidgen too young. I wondered what my students would discover, thirty years later.

I recommend this exercise to anyone interested in stirring up the emotions of citizenship. For more than what the assignment did for me was what it did for my students. The stories were captivating. Most of the students interviewed parents or relatives, discovering that a conversation about voting inevitably turned into a conversation about something else: motivation, identity, belief. Not all the tales were draped in red, white, and blue—Paul Townsend said that his father voted in '72 simply because his girlfriend at the time threatened to break up with him if he didn't. And, of course, half the newly eligible voters nationwide did not cast a ballot.

But for many it was, in the words of Marc Williams's aunt, "an unexpected coming of age," a time of empowerment and hope. As Erin Wilson's mother said, "I was proud as a young African American to be able to vote. I felt as though the things that had been fought for and struggled for had been achieved, at least on paper."

For a few short years, all eyes were on that generation, from which much was expected, and much given in return. It's a lesson to anyone looking for ways to rekindle that civic passion in young people today.

As the Twenty-sixth Amendment raced through the fastest ratification process in history—three months and seven days—analysts wondered how the influx of millions of new voters would affect the political equation, and politicians worried about how they would now conduct business, particularly in and around college towns. Just days after Ohio's historic vote, R. W. Apple, writing in the *New York Times,* observed that "in the last three months, more and more politicians have decided that this change is different, and that it could make old styles obsolete. . . . There are those who continue to believe that the impact of the youth vote will be marginal. But they are a minority."

Instead, almost immediately, politicians scrambled to take into account what became known as "the kid factor." Senator Edmund S. Muskie, a centrist Democrat from Maine running for president, began tailoring his message to the young, even if it hurt him with his older, right-of-center constituency. The uncompromising views of Eugene McCarthy on the left and George Wallace on the right were thought to appeal to younger voters unappreciative of the middle-of-the-road nature of most politicians.

Massive rallies were held to register the millions of citizens now suddenly eligible to vote. Five thousand youths jammed into New York's Central Park during one such gathering, more rock concert than civics class, as the casts of the Broadway musicals *Hair* and *The Me Nobody Knows* serenaded the crowd. The message was unmistakable. A generation had awakened.

"It's wonderful to register, to have a voice in politics, because everything the government does affects our nation," an eighteen-year-old student named Sharon Quille told the *New York Times*.

Indeed, as soon as the legislation enfranchising eighteen-year-olds passed the Congress, before it even morphed into a constitutional amendment, voter registration became an overnight sensation. A few weeks before Ohio's dramatic vote on the amendment, *Newsweek* was reporting on this nationwide trend under the headline "A Quiet Revolution?" in its June 14, 1971, edition:

> At Woodrow Wilson High School in San Francisco last week, senior students were called into a morning assembly to hear about the importance of registration and voting in a democracy. It was the same sort of civics lesson American schools have conducted for generations but it had a new finale: after the lecture, the students filed over to tables where county voting registrars were waiting to sign them up on the spot. Imaginative campaigns like the one at Woodrow Wilson are now being run in scores of cities from coast to coast....
>
> At stake for 1972 are some 25 million potential first-time Presidential voters—not just the newly enfranchised 18-through-20-year-olds but 13.6 million others who will have turned 21 since the '68 election. The importance of a group this size in another close Presidential election can hardly be ignored. And, depending upon ratification of the proposed 26th Amendment and passage of various state voting laws, the young voters could have a sizable impact in state and local elections.

Everyone was getting into the act. Major labor unions, civic and civil rights groups, youth activist coalitions, the League of

Women Voters, National Urban League, Southern Christian Leadership Council, Democratic National Committee, Republican National Committee—all mounted vigorous efforts to sign up new voters, especially new young voters. Eager registrars armed with clipboards, the proper forms, and an inexhaustible supply of enthusiasm went door-to-door and set up folding tables anywhere they could. Organizers were seeking permission to do what officials did at Woodrow Wilson High—send volunteer registrars into high schools. Allard Lowenstein, the liberal activist par excellence, organized what he called "Registration Summer" in 1971, a nonpartisan movement to rouse young voters against the Vietnam War with rallies in dozens of states.

But as with every attempt to extend the franchise in American history, this movement to enlist new voters was mightily opposed on many fronts. Even the eventual passage and ratification of the Twenty-sixth Amendment did not prevent the give-and-take-away dynamic from recurring. As *Newsweek* noted, "The most controversial question is no longer whether young people should vote but where."

Although 60 percent of the newly enfranchised young people were out of school and at work, the 40 percent in college commanded a lion's share of attention and aggravation. Should students be allowed to register and vote where they attend school, or only where their parents live?

Across the country was a crazy quilt of regulations and customs, which in some cases differed from town to town. A few examples:

• Married students on campus at Princeton University were able to vote there, but single students were not.
• A Harvard student on full scholarship could vote locally, but one who still received support from home could vote only at home.

• A graduate student at Yale University was not allowed to register to vote, but his wife was—because she wasn't a student.

Beyond these idiosyncratic examples of discrimination were huge discrepancies in state law. When the Twenty-sixth Amendment became permanently attached to the Constitution, thirty-four states had their own laws making it difficult or impossible for students to register at college. Twelve required that young people be financially independent. Eleven categorically excluded students from town politics; eleven others had partial restrictions. Senator Edward Kennedy, who had introduced legislation to federalize registration, decried what he called "an arbitrary, obsolete, and unfair system by which vast numbers of Americans are silenced at the polls."

Intoned *The New Republic*: "The 26th Amendment extended to young people an invitation to participate in national political life. Given the evident political leanings of the young (many more Democrat or Independent than Republican), it's not surprising that middle-aged conservative politicians and the pillars of local community might wish to withdraw the welcome. But it's late for that."

There was, however, more to this issue. *Newsweek* noted that a Gallup poll showed that two out of three Americans opposed students voting in the communities that hosted their colleges and universities—but not necessarily because the young were wide-eyed radicals. "Around the country," the newsmagazine reported on August 30, 1971, "a survey found that much of the opposition is based on a vision of the student as a non-taxpaying passerby whose idealism—rather than his frivolity or Berkeley-style radicalism—threatens the long-run stability of the community. 'They float a bond issue and then move on, and who's left holding the bag?' argues New Hampshire Attorney General Warren Rudman."

Warren Rudman went on to a distinguished career as a U.S.

senator and then as a corporate ethics guru; the trend he so worried about largely did not materialize. In March 1972, the U.S. Supreme Court ruled that state laws requiring a long period of residency as a condition for voting are unconstitutional, and that registration books may be closed only a brief time before Election Day itself—generally no longer than thirty days. So students were allowed to register in their more temporary abodes, but never did so in numbers large and consistent enough to turn local politics inside out.

Another worried prediction on the part of conservatives also did not materialize: a 1972 Democratic victory based on a swelling of the Democratic rolls. Helped by the influx of young voters and blacks from the South, the number of Americans registered as Democrats just about matched the number calling themselves Republicans—a first in decades. "Nonwhites and young citizens are population segments where the McGovern forces expect to pick up millions of votes," *U.S. News & World Report* wrote about the prospects of Democratic nominee George McGovern in the summer of '72.

Instead, Richard Nixon won reelection with more than 60 percent of the popular vote and an Electoral College victory so lopsided that only the state of Massachusetts fell in the Democratic column. It appears that many young voters, like the rest of the country, approved of Nixon's hard line on the Vietnam War, his diplomatic overtures to the Soviet Union and China, and his domestic leadership more than they could embrace McGovern's error-prone campaign and more liberal platform.

But one concern raised back in the summer of '72 has proven to be eerily predictive: It was difficult to register to vote then, and it still is today. It's fascinating in light of all the surveys and studies done recently to read a story published more than three decades ago outlining the very same obstacles. In August 1972 *U.S. News & World Report* asked the question "Why is the job of registering people to vote so difficult?"—and then proceeded to provide a litany of now-familiar answers. Just getting to the registration offices was difficult. Voters lacked transportation, or they weren't able to leave work, or the hours of registration office operation made it cumbersome to get there on time. The few employees in these offices were overworked. Local politicians were reluctant to add to the roles new voters with unknown or unpredictable allegiances.

"Often," the magazine reported, "the only place to register in a big city is a central office of the elections board or a city hall.... [T]he complaint is made that it all adds up to much inconvenience—too much for many people."

Nonetheless, nearly half the voters aged eighteen to twenty-four cast a ballot in that election, even though polls showed that the outcome was hardly in doubt. When my students at the University of Pennsylvania related the stories gleaned from interviewing some of those first-time voters, it was clear that—despite protestations to the contrary—many of these adults could easily reach back thirty years and recall specific details of the experience. It was that important. Rachel Kreinces interviewed a family friend who first shrugged and said the day was "no big deal." Then he went on to describe the very look and smell of the voting booth—the old and odorous curtain that afforded privacy to this most private act; the darkness of the voting booth; the sluggishness of the poll workers. So slow were they that he had to write his name upside down in the ledger because they could not command the energy to turn it around for each voter.

It was also clear that motivation, passion, and purpose were chasing them to the ballot box, despite whatever obstacles were placed in their way.

Opposition to the Vietnam War and to the Nixon presidency provided the motivation, passion, and purpose for many. "Anne Kerzner cast her ballot for the first time in Yaphank, New York, in the fall of 1972," wrote Dan Koken, one of my students. "At that time, Anne was an 18-year-old college freshman with passionate liberal ideals and a wish to be heard as an adult through the voting booth. She entered that voting booth with hopes of removing President Nixon from office and getting a Democrat like George McGovern in the White House. This plan of hers failed, but she still relished the experience."

Kerzner, a friend of Koken's family, described the rush of excitement at that time, as if everything was done in the plural. "Anne and her friends all headed off to the voting booths, wide-eyed and optimistic about their opportunity to voice their opinion. Anne talked about the interest in politics that the Vietnam War had spurred in young people of her generation and the effect that Vietnam had on their political views. Anne and her peers believed that if they were old enough to be drafted, they deserved to vote. They had earned what they considered to be an obvious right in the passage of the 26th Amendment, and they refused to squander this opportunity."

Michael Schimmel's father was another voter propelled to select a candidate because of the war. An eighteen-year-old freshman at Emerson College in Boston in 1972, Kurt Schimmel told his son that all of his peers voted that year, thrilled at being the first generation to be able to do so at such a young age. More than the novelty of the vote was the sense of actual power they felt by participating in the process. It made a lasting impression on many of them: Kurt Schimmel has never missed an election since. Subsequently a lifelong Republican, he voted for McGovern that one time. The war made him do it. Hearing the story left Michael wondering whether it will take another Vietnam— "or worse"—to drive his generation to the polls.

For many of these first-timers, walking into the voting

booth was the culmination, not the start, of political engagement. Prohibited from attending nighttime vigils and noisy rallies because of her father's high-security clearance for his job, Kate Liberman's mother instead stayed home and wrote passionate letters to the president, articulating her views on the war. Consequently, the opportunity to vote as an eighteen-year-old in 1972 was a long-awaited thrill. "The new right of suffrage was more than simply a vote," Liberman wrote of her mother's experience, "it was the chance and privilege to express her views with the rest of the American community."

So, too, for Deirdre Connolly's mother, a political activist at her alma mater, Trenton State, who had already organized rallies against the Vietnam War and marched on Washington before the Twenty-sixth Amendment gave her, at nineteen, the right to vote. "Engulfed in the politically vibrant milieu of the era," Connolly wrote, "she remembered the time as one of idealism and participation with peers."

For some, the moment became so embedded in their psyche that they clutched it like a talisman into adulthood. Perhaps it should be no surprise that Kate Liberman's mother became a die-hard voter, and that she still has a scrapbook with her voter registration card, McGovern flyers, and a *Time* magazine story of the 1972 election—like a time capsule from a distant era. Deirdre Connolly's mother had the opposite reaction. Turned off by the hypocrisy of both the politicians and the antiwar movement, disappointed in the outcome of the election, her enthusiasm for the political process waned. After 1972, she never voted again.

The adults interviewed by these Penn students were hardly a representative sample of the American electorate since most (though not all) chose McGovern over Nixon. Their overall commitment to the democratic process—or, at least, how they explained it years later to the young men and women of my class—also was probably not the norm, even during those activist times. Voting was, in Nicolas Walter's father's words, not a "symbolic rite of passage or honor, but rather an affirmation of a basic right that all Americans should have." William Walters knew that his candidate wouldn't win, but voted for McGovern anyway, for a very concrete reason: "My father felt that since Nixon's election was essentially assured, that he should vote for McGovern just to make a statement. Dad also thought that the two-party system would be jeopardized if Nixon won every state, and more than two-thirds of the popular vote. So in a way, that election of 1972 was a defining one for my father because he felt as though his vote was more significant than it has been for the presidential elections since then."

One theme emerging from many of these stories remains a powerful predictor today in determining a young person's civic and political engagement: the role of the family. In the way that research often confirms what we already know, contemporary studies have proven that a young person is more likely to vote if his or her parents vote. Those studies weren't available back in 1972, but many parents obviously knew the truth intuitively.

Student after student had a story to tell of family pressure, persuasion, and tradition on Election Day. Chun Shin, who became a citizen only a few years ago, interviewed a psychiatrist who had grown up in the Philadelphia suburbs and attended the University of Pennsylvania. Her mother had personally traveled to the Penn campus to go with her to register to vote. It was that important. Paul Townsend's mother recalled that even though the absentee ballot process was a hassle for a young woman away from home, she knew she had to do it; her parents would never forgive her if she didn't vote. Erin Wilson's mother, Michele—like her daughter, a Penn student from Philadelphia—went home and voted with her own mother that day. Erin picks up the story:

"It was somewhat of a tradition starting when she was younger, when she accompanied my grandmother to the polls. (I also was subject to the same ritual as a child.) This was the initial exposure she had to the process, and arguably the most important. It helped her recognize voting as an obligation to the community."

Erin Wilson is African American. Marc Williams comes from a large, Italian immigrant family. The same rules applied.

Voting, Williams wrote, "was seen as an amplification of our family's political voice. Unusually cohesive (even for an Italian family), they faced all their battles (mainly financial ones) as a team. With such a mind-set, family unity represented a natural approach to the fierce world of politics. My aunt fondly recalls walking with her parents and grandfather to the local polling place, a fire hall just blocks away, after coming home from work. 'We savored the moment,' she recounts. 'We did it as a group, and it was special.'"

Marc Williams's aunt didn't vote merely as an individual, but as a daughter and granddaughter carrying out a tradition that pervaded her family's life as much as the food they ate and the holidays they celebrated. Their political party affiliation was no secret; Williams's great-grandfather hung two portraits over his bed from 1960 until the day he died—Jesus Christ and John F. Kennedy. The Twenty-sixth Amendment was not just an abstract victory for a rowdy generation, but a direct way to find another vote in the family for "the good guys."

Context was everything for these new voters. There was no question in their minds that the adults in their lives wanted them to participate, in stark contrast to today's situation. Research tells us that one of the strongest reasons Americans in general, and young people in particular, cast a ballot is that the people they value also value voting. It's peer pressure of a grander sort. That's what was going on in 1972, and that's not what is going on enough today.

Listen to Jimmy Christianson's story:

My mother (Annmarie) was 18 years old and a senior at Oceanside High School on Long Island in 1971.... She never involved herself in the protests because she was neither a vocal nor outgoing individual. But deep down inside she believed that if 18-year-olds were old enough to die for their country, then they were definitely old enough to vote for their representatives. "We could smoke cigarettes and drink alcohol at 18, as well as die for our country, but not vote? It was absurd. We needed the right to have a say in our lives, and not just let the politicians that we didn't elect make the decisions for us.

"The Board of Elections actually came to the high school in the spring of 1972 for a week to register the new voters. Nobody was forced to register," Annmarie said, "but everyone I knew did it...."

I attended the same high school as my mother 20 years later, and many of the issues she spoke about and faced were absent during my tenure. First of all, the Board of Elections didn't spend a week, let alone a minute, coming to my high school to register new voters. The only controversial topics students protested were grades, not war or inherent rights. Even with the election of 2000 being as tight and insane as it was, there wasn't a feeling that we needed to go to the voting booth.

Ben Cruse made a similarly rueful observation after talking with several people who had come of age in 1972. "As I sat down to reflect on the things I heard throughout my interviews, I noticed one strand that went through each and it disturbed me," Cruse wrote. "The common theme was that each one of these people, as they all hovered around the age of 50, accepted the fact that America's youth (and Americans in general) don't vote. They did not dispute it, nor attempt to defend our nation's youth or the political system on which we ride. They offered no solutions, but approached the topic as a foregone conclusion.

"Perhaps it is time that we shake off the apathy, and finally begin to wonder why our youth choose not to vote."

CHAPTER FOUR

Knock the Vote:
Why young people don't vote today, and why the political establishment wants it that way

It was an offhand comment, candid and revealing. Brian Tierney, the campaign manager for Republican Sam Katz's quest to become mayor of Philadelphia in 2003, was relating a conversation he had had with a political consultant about two months before Election Day. They were looking at numbers—registrations, turnout, the nitty-gritty fundamentals of Philadelphia's politics—and Tierney pointed to the "Under 30" column.

"What about these?" he asks.

"Don't worry," the consultant says, "they're not going to vote. You don't want to spend a lot of time talking about things that matter to people who don't vote."

There, in a nutshell, is the bald truth of today's generational politics: Young people don't vote, so candidates don't talk about their issues, so they become further disillusioned with the process and stay away in greater numbers. It's a vicious cycle that makes plenty of sense if you are a candidate with limited resources of time and money, but only serves to further widen the gap—no, the canyon—now developing between young people and the public officials who are supposed to serve them.

But don't take my word for it. Listen to Sean "P. Diddy" Combs, recording artist, Grammy-winning producer and bad boy business mogul. Here's what he wrote for a book entitled *Crossroads: The Future of American Politics*:

Young people don't vote. It's sad to hear that, but it's true. Young people just don't get out there to the polls in the numbers they should. They realize not voting is going to keep them frustrated and without power. The problem is that there's no one to vote for. Republicans and Democrats speak a good game—when asked about what they're doing to appeal to young people they'll spit chapter and verse about their record on education and social services—but in reality, politicians have given up on the kids. And so, in return, kids have given up on them....

This mentality runs rampant through the minds of young people, both black and white, rich and poor. It doesn't matter if you live in the 'hood or the suburbs. Nine times out of ten, you're going to believe—most of the time with good reason—that politics, and politicians, do not exist to serve any of your best interests. This is why young people feel so disenfranchised.

The trend has not escaped the attention of the academic world, and there are now a growing number of scholars examining why this is happening and what it means. One of them is Martin P. Wattenberg, a professor of political science at the University of California at Irvine and author of *Where Have All the Voters Gone?* In a long opinion piece in the September 21, 2003, *Boston Globe* he wrote:

If one had to choose a single word to describe the current relationship between candidates and young citizens it would be "neglect." Politicians know who their customers are. Why should they worry about young non-voters any more than the makers of denture cream worry about people with healthy teeth ...?

If election observers at Iraq's first post-Saddam election noticed that older people were voting at twice the rates of younger people, it would be pronounced a severe problem. Here in the United States, we are so accustomed to this pattern that it hardly attracts notice.

In one sense, the pattern is as old as the Republic. Younger voters—however that age is defined—have long been expected to vote and engage politically in lower numbers than their elders. Youth is a temporary state of citizenship; unlike formerly disenfranchised groups such as women and blacks, who can never change or grow out of their gender and race, young voters are simply not young forever. Age is a fleeting civic characteristic, shaping an outlook on politics that we expect to alter with time. A twenty-year-old college student may have less in common with a thirty-year-old married, home-owning, lawn-mowing father than the older man may have with his own father. The disconnect is especially pronounced when it comes to local politics, which tends to center on issues—taxes, schools, zoning—that have little to do with the lives of many young people. I remember as a twenty-something, unmarried newspaper reporter in a small town in Connecticut being sent to cover a zoning commission and thinking that I may as well be covering life on Mars, it seemed that foreign.

But this disconnect exists profoundly in national politics, too. Mark S. Mellman, president of The Mellman Group in Washington, D.C., has worked for Democratic candidates and causes since 1982, and makes it his business to understand generational attitudes toward political issues. "If you look down a list of issues, for older people it's health care," Mellman says. "For people between thirty and fifty, it's education for their kids. Below thirty, it's all over the map. It's much harder to devise an issue-based strategy for young people." In his view, the contrast with the elderly is striking: "By old age, your age identifies a sense of needs. You are older longer than you are younger. Unless it ends, you don't remain young for the rest of your life."

In fact, some argue that the decline in voter turnout during the last four decades in America can be explained largely by a generational divide, or what Peter Beinart of *The New Republic* calls the "age gap." In the 1992 and 1996 presidential elections, for instance, the two most common demographic features of nonvoters were residential mobility and youth. So if you were young and if you moved within the last two years (a feature of the young), you were far less likely to vote than anyone else.

This explanation especially resonates when examining the trends in midterm elections, the true test of voting behavior. The Committee for the Study of the American Electorate regularly produces exhaustive reports analyzing every inch of the national electoral profile, and it doesn't take a statistician to pick out this trend from the CSAE's raff of numbers. Since 1974, when eighteen-year-olds were first allowed to vote in midterm elections, turnout for the younger cohort of Americans is much lower than for their parents' and grandparents' generation. How much lower?

1974: 24 percent for 18- to 24-year-olds; 57 percent for 45- to 64-year-olds

1986: 22 percent for 18- to 24-year-olds; 61 percent for those older than 65

1998: 17 percent for 18- to 24-year-olds; nearly 60 percent for those older than 65.

A word about these numbers. For years, turnout was thought to be a simple calculation in which the numerator is the number of votes cast and the denominator is the number of Americans eligible to vote. That last percentage for 1998 was based on the Census Bureau's biennial estimates of what is called the VAP, the Voting Age Population. Some political scientists and researchers are comfortable using the VAP, because they believe that the comparison to the entire adult population reflects the real measure of civic participation. But lately many other scholars have come to realize that there are serious flaws in this calculation, since it includes many segments of the population who may be eligible to vote because they are eighteen or older but are ineligible for other reasons.

For one thing, the VAP includes felons, and in thirty-six

states felons temporarily lose their voting rights; in twelve states they lose them for good. It includes noncitizens, who are not permitted to vote. It includes a small number of people deemed incompetent to vote who reside in mental institutions. It includes those who cannot vote because they didn't meet the residency requirement for that election. And it does *not* include those Americans living abroad who are technically able to vote by absentee ballot.

The practical impact of this calculation is profound. Including noncitizens, the mobile, and the young makes the turnout picture much bleaker in states like California, Florida, and New York. But changing that pesky denominator has not been a straightforward task. Should it count only registered voters? All citizens? And how does it take into account a fluid population like felons, whose franchise status varies from state to state, and the expatriates who may move back and forth from our shores?

In the last couple of years, a consensus has emerged among researchers that bases the denominator solely on citizenship. Although not a perfect solution, it has the virtue of being reasonable and easy to calculate. Meantime, many of the number crunchers believe that the number of felons (who cannot vote) and the number of expats (who can) roughly cancel each other out.

The consequence of this change in calculation is that American democracy looks slightly more respectable than it did using the old figures. But not by much. According to the CSAE, if the new formula is applied nationally, the turnout rate of eligible citizens in the 2000 presidential election was actually 52.7 percent, as opposed to 50.1 percent based on the now discredited VAP. Doing similar math on the 1998 midterm elections pulls the turnout to 37.1 percent, compared to 35.3 percent.

Only in modern-day America would this look like good news—that nearly half the eligible voters stayed home in 2000 for one of the closest and most disputed elections in the nation's history. Remember, too, that since Americans are not required to state their ages when they vote, all these calculations are based on polling and surveys that ask people *whether* they voted. So, human nature being what it is, in a system based on self-reporting the numbers are very likely inflated. Indeed, studies have shown that 8 to 10 percent of Americans interviewed misreport their voting habits by claiming to vote when, in fact, they have not. Among those who would like credit for casting a ballot without having to do the actual deed, the young are among the biggest offenders.

Meantime, even the slight uptick earned by this new calculation doesn't obliterate the fact that voting among the young is low and slipping fast, faster than the decline in voting among older groups. Mark Hugo Lopez, who as the research director of the Center for Information and Research on Civic Learning and Engagement (CIRCLE) is the acknowledged keeper of wisdom and guru of graphs, entitles his recent paper on this subject, "Youth Voter Turnout Has Declined, By Any Measure."

The debate about the denominator is beside the point, Lopez and coauthor Peter Levine argue: "Whether we measure the percentage of young residents who vote, or the percentage of young citizens who vote, the decline is substantial." While overall turnout in presidential elections has declined since 1972 by about 4 percent, the drop for the eighteen- to twenty-one-year-old voting cohort is between 13 and 15 percent, depending on which calculation is used.

None of the actual numbers, Levine and Lopez write, "should be used to derive a precise turnout rate for young people in any given year, because our data come from surveys, which always inflate levels of participation. The only thing we know for sure is that the rate of youth participation has declined since 1972—by any reasonable measure."

Why? Certain factors are depressing voter turnout regardless of age, but like wily diseases that know how to pick on the most vulnerable, they hurt the young more aggressively.

"The great tools of democracy—its electoral institutions and media organizations—have increasingly been used for private agency," Thomas E. Patterson writes in *The Vanishing Voter*. "Personal ambition now drives campaigns, and profit and celebrity now drive journalism. Candidates, public officials, and journalists operate in a narrow professional world that is largely of their own making and that is remote from the world of the public they serve." This sea change in American democracy may create a kind of dissonance with the Greatest Generation, who came of age through the Depression and a world war and looked to their leaders and civic institutions with attachment and pride. It may also create a disconnect with baby boomers, whose political empowerment in the 1960s and 1970s is a not-so-distant memory.

But these older generations still retain a sense of politics as it once was. Young people can't cling to that memory and that motivation because they never had them in the first place. The nature of politics has changed from a participatory to a spectator sport. Young people see it as a war waged on television, loaded with negative ads and *gotcha* stories that seem dirty and distasteful, especially if they've never met a real candidate. Patterson's Vanishing Voter project at Harvard University conducted 80,000 interviews to uncover and understand the source of voter discontent. Traditionally, the nonvoter has fallen into three categories: they are alienated from politics, apathetic and bored, or disconnected because of age or disability. But the project revealed a new type of nonvoter: the disenchanted. "They are the nonvoters who have been spawned by the political gamesmanship and negative news that dominated late-twentieth-century politics," he writes. "Many of them express interest in public affairs, talk occasionally about politics, and keep up with the news. In fact, the Vanishing Voter surveys show they do not differ greatly from voters in these respects. Nor do they differ significantly from voters in terms of years of education. Where they differ is in their disgust with the way that politics in the United States is conducted, which leads some of them to stay away from the polls on Election Day."

And, no surprise here, that new type of voter is heavily concentrated among the young, because political mistrust and disengagement is cumulative. It builds through time, through years of television watching and secondhand civic experiences. Even the most defining event in the lives of America's young— the terrorist attacks of September 11, 2001—was, in most of the nation, experienced chiefly through television. The negative messages that have rained down on the young and created this profound mistrust of politics were never cushioned by or contrasted with other political experiences. And so, more than ever, they have translated this mistrust into doing something on Election Day other than voting.

"Our generation has not experienced government as it can, should and does exist," write Ganesh Sitaraman and Previn Warren in *Invisible Citizens*. "We face instead a version of politics that is bureaucratic, disengaged and distasteful—a negative political culture part reality and part fantasy, part historical truth and part media-driven illusion."

The disengagement may be even more dramatic for those who have not been historically embraced by the political system. Martrice Candler explored these feelings in an emotional essay published in *Bay View,* a black newspaper based in San Francisco, in October 2003. "In the 2000 Presidential election, watching the candidates run for office made me queasy," she writes. "I always felt that the persona the candidates portrayed in their advertisements were artificial and that the media focus was limited and slanted.... As a young woman of color, I felt I was receiving a subliminal message not to vote at all."

But disengagement isn't just about feelings. Some of the

messages delivered by candidates have been loud and clear. The absence of young people from the political process, combined with the outsized influence played by interest group lobbying, often means that issues important to many younger citizens are pushed aside by those issues important to a narrow but vocal and active set of (usually older) voters. This is why the national discussion of health care is obsessed with prescription drug coverage—for the elderly, of course—and ignores the fact that most young people want basic benefits they can take with them from place to place. This is also why the issue of "education" is largely framed from the perspective of baby boomers, concerned about the schooling received by their children and the burden it places on their taxes. But that is not necessarily "education" as defined by young people, who actually sit in dilapidated classrooms or have to pay back the sky-high rates of college tuition for years to come.

Here's how this disconnect plays out: In a Gallup poll conducted a year before the 2004 presidential election, Americans in the eighteen- to twenty-nine-year-old group tended to rate issues that would directly affect their lives—education, jobs, the economy—as more important than terrorism, the situation in Iraq, health care, and taxes. But terrorism, health care, and taxes are the priorities of older people, and therefore the priorities of Congress and the White House. This is why the United States is a nation where poverty among the elderly was addressed by Medicare and Social Security decades ago, and poverty among children remains a persistent and shameful reality.

The greatest disconnect with young people may be found in social issues. A CNN/USA Today poll in October 2003 found that a majority of young Americans—53 percent—support same-sex marriages that are recognized with equal rights under the law, while only 32 percent in the older group backed such a concept. The survey also asked whether racial and ethnic minorities should be encouraged to maintain their own culture or blend into the larger American society, and the gap was similarly huge: 54 percent of younger Americans but only 32 percent of older ones favored ethnic diversity over homogeneity.

You can appreciate how the political world just doesn't seem relevant to the average college sophomore or Wal-Mart associate. No wonder, then, that when *American Prospect* magazine issued in October 2003 what it called a Contract with America's Youth—"the essential needs of the next generation"—few of the items on the list laced the conversations of most of the presidential candidates at the time.

This hasn't stopped the candidates from trying to woo the vast, up-for-grabs pool of youth voters, but their attempts draw mixed reviews. The first-ever collaboration between the ultra-hip Rock the Vote and CNN produced a televised debate of the Democratic presidential candidates on Election Day 2003 that did reach more viewers than any previous debate. And the under-thirty questioners and audience liked the informal ambience—candidates sitting on stools instead of standing behind podiums, surrounded on all sides in a sort of debate-in-the-round. Much of the audience dressed down, and so did many of the candidates, some shedding their ties and jackets as soon as they arrived, others choosing to leave them at home altogether. But the debate was criticized once it was revealed that a CNN producer fed one student, a freshman at Brown University, a rather silly question about whether the candidates preferred Macs or PCs. The student was rebuffed when she presented a more intelligent version of the question, told it wasn't light-hearted enough for the debate's demographic.

An editorial in the *Brown Daily Herald* expressed the students' feelings: "In the future, media outlets should realize that sensible, reasoned debate, not lame jokes, is the way to attract potential young voters. We know when we're being pandered to. And we don't like it."

Remember, this is a generation weaned on slick marketing

by master manipulators. They can detect an attempt to patronize moments after it hits the airwaves, and they will easily become suspicious when John Kerry rides a Harley-Davidson onto the stage of *The Tonight Show* or Wesley Clark shows up in a mock turtleneck to the CNN debate. After that debate, Rock the Vote challenged each Democrat to produce a 30-second video that would encourage young people to vote and posted them on its website. Kate Liberman, a freshman in my Penn class, analyzed the videos with the ease and precision of an accomplished scientist and concluded that "the videos whose goal was simply to encourage young voters to register are less effective than those in which the candidates present their views on important issues to young voters."

Kate panned Dennis Kucinich's presentation because it was all rap music and no policy, John Edwards's clip because he used the word *they* when talking about young people ("I could not relate as he was not talking *to* me but about me," she observed), and several others who described themselves simply as the anti-Bush. Yet when John Kerry and Joe Lieberman presented their respective platforms with a degree of specificity and substance, Kate could relate. "Hearing a candidate's policies and goals, I was galvanized to vote," she decided.

Without realizing it, perhaps, Kate Liberman was expressing more than her own opinion; she was reflecting a generational attitude. In a "toolkit" for candidates and campaign staff designed to encourage them to understand, reach, and turn out young voters, the Center for Democracy and Citizenship lists various myths and then counters them with fact:

MYTH: Young voters will tune you out if you're not hip or cool.
REALITY: Young voters crave authenticity and honesty. . . . In their voting decisions, young voters rely much more on serious, hard qualities—your stands on the issues, your record, and your

expertise—than on soft qualities, like your appearance and manner. You'll connect best with young voters by listening to them and taking them seriously. Don't dress or act differently for them—they smell phoniness a mile away.

Obviously, the folks who advise candidates to shun ties, ride motorcycles, and produce rap music videos haven't yet gotten the message.

* * *

This disconnect is only worsened by the mechanics of voting in a nation that has long been proud to extend the franchise on paper but quite adept at limiting it in practice. Like poll taxes and literacy tests, the de facto obstacles to voting are not written specifically with the young in mind, but there's no mistaking that the young are disproportionately affected.

Simply put, voting is cumbersome when you're young and shuttling between home and college, or home and the military, and don't feel connected to any one place. The mobility that characterizes this generation makes it hard for them to vote, and the governing rules and regulations don't make it easy.

Just registering to vote can be an ordeal. Although the Motor Voter initiative in 1993, which allowed citizens to register at state motor vehicle agencies, did boost the roles, the initial surge didn't last. And there's been enough research by now to know what does work for young people. Unfortunately, those in control of the process, especially state officials, aren't listening and the clamor for reform isn't growing any louder.

For instance, solid research and plenty of anecdotal evidence has shown that allowing voters to register on Election Day draws more young people into the process. In a paper published by CIRCLE in February 2003, Mary Fitzgerald of Mary Washington University wrote that "Election Day registration

boosts youth voting activity in presidential elections by an estimated 14 percentage points, and by an estimated 4 percentage
points in midterm congressional elections, even when control-
ling for contact by political parties." Jesse Ventura might not
have known the actual survey data, but he sure was familiar
with the consequences—young male Minnesotans who registered to vote on Election Day were credited with helping the
gruff, wrestler Independent snatch the governor's job in 1998.

Yet along with Minnesota, only six other states—Idaho,
Maine, New Hampshire, Oregon, Wisconsin, and Wyoming—
allow Election Day registration. The fears that loosening the
rules will usher in fraud and corruption have not been borne
out. Instead, in the 2000 election, 68 percent of the eligible population voted in those six states, compared with 53 percent in
the rest of the country. Still, most of the nation sticks to a system that we know sets up subtle but effective roadblocks on the
road to a fuller democracy.

There's more. Seven states require a new voter to be present
in his home district the first time he votes—Illinois, Michigan,
Louisiana, Nevada, Tennessee, Virginia, and West Virginia. So
if a student turns eighteen in the spring of her senior year in
high school and goes away to college in the fall, she is effectively
disenfranchised from voting unless she can show up, in person,
at home, on Election Day.

And in the majority of states that do allow first-time voters
to cast a ballot from afar, securing that ballot can be an ar-
duous task. In my home state of Pennsylvania, for example, my
college-age daughter had to fill out an application for the absentee ballot, send it in, wait for the ballot, fill that out and send
it back in time to be counted in the election. All this presumes
that she a) checks her mailbox regularly and b) has a few postage
stamps—not easy assumptions to make about college students.
College students today live in an electronic cyberworld; they

don't use envelopes and stamps as we might have at their age. I once asked students in an upper-level seminar at the University of Pennsylvania why more of them didn't file absentee ballots and the most common response was that they didn't have postage stamps. This from a bunch of political science majors living a few blocks from Philadelphia's central post office.

We can judge them as apathetic or lazy. Or we can realize that the system as it now stands does not fit into the rhythms of their lives and that if we want them to vote, it would not take much to bend the system to make the act of voting more attractive. Consider: A survey conducted by the U.S. Census found that younger adults were more likely than older adults to report that they did not vote in the 2000 presidential election because they were too busy or had conflicting work or school schedules. We can shrug and further alienate them from this essential act of citizenship, or we can recognize that there are concrete ways to make the actual process of voting easier and more accessible—for the young and, indeed, for everyone.

We should also teach young people *how* to vote. The annual poll conducted by Harvard University's Institute of Politics (IOP) is sometimes criticized for surveying only students in four-year colleges, hardly a representative sample of all Americans in that age group. Still, even these presumably educated, motivated students show an alarming ignorance of the mechanics of voting. Of those who indicated that they planned to vote in the 2004 presidential election, more than one-quarter— 26 percent—said that they don't know or "aren't sure" where their polling place is or how to vote by absentee ballot. "The biggest single predictor of those who are unsure of how to vote is age," says the IOP report—that is, first-year students under the age of eighteen. In other words, students who have just graduated from high school and just left home. School and home—the two predominant influences in these young people's lives have failed to teach them how to use the basic tool of citizenship.

"Politicians are fond of urging the young not to be so apathetic," Peter Beinart wrote in *The New Republic*. "But their admonitions would carry more weight if they addressed the structural barriers that feed that indifference."

The third, and most damning, reason for the dramatic decline in youth turnout is related to the shrinking allegiance of the young to the established Democratic and Republican parties. A central tenet of American political behavior is that— young or old—those who identify more strongly with either political party are more likely to vote. When that sense of identity fades, so does voting and many other forms of substantive political participation.

This didn't occur overnight; the parties' hold on the American electorate has been loosening for nearly a hundred years. In the late nineteenth century, 70 percent and sometimes 80 percent of the eligible population went to the polls to elect a president, a turnout that America has not witnessed since 1900. (And this was at a time when huge swaths of the black population in the South were effectively disenfranchised.) One persuasive theory for the rise and fall in voting has been its association with the rise and fall of the strength and pervasiveness of political parties. In their omnibus book *American Government*, James Q. Wilson and John J. Dilulio Jr. note that during the nineteenth century, according to this theory, "the parties fought hard, worked strenuously to get as many voters as possible to the polls, afforded the mass of voters a chance to participate in party politics through caucuses and conventions, kept the legal barriers to participation low, and looked forward to close, exciting elections."

But once the new century dawned, party competitiveness waned as national elections usually resulted in lopsided victories. Citizens began losing interest in politics and the parties themselves were less interested in mobilizing the mass of voters than in maintaining their tight hold on the reigns of power and perceived influence. (Never mind that they were also, sometimes rightly, accused of corruption and backroom manipulation.) The trend accelerated after the tumultuous 1960s, as Robert Putnam showed in his acclaimed work *Bowling Alone.* Party identification, the voters' sense of commitment to his or her own team, fell from more than 75 percent around 1960 to less than 65 percent in the late 1990s, his research showed. Despite a partial recovery in the late 1980s, party "brand loyalty" remained well below the levels of the 1950s and early 1960s. And the trend lines are not promising: As older, more partisan voters depart from the electorate, they are replaced by younger independents, and the net attachment to parties is likely to continue to decline. "Again, the Grim Reaper is silently at work, lowering political involvement," Putnam writes ominously.

It makes perfect political sense for parties to direct their precious resources of time, money, and creativity to woo the most predictable voters. And young people are not predictable, exhibiting a growing streak of political independence that shows them to be less ideological than their elders. A 2002 survey of 1,500 young people by Lake Snell, Perry & Associates and the Tarrance Group found that 30 percent called themselves Democrats, 28 percent Republicans, and 27 percent Independents. (They were also similarly split between conservative, moderate, and liberal.) Among four-year college students surveyed in the annual Harvard poll, the number calling themselves Independents has surged ahead of the number claiming allegiance to either political party. In the April 2000 poll, 33 percent deemed themselves Independent or unaffiliated. By April 2004, the number had risen to 41 percent—rushing ahead of the Democrats (32 percent) and the Republicans (24 percent).

This doesn't necessarily mean that these young independents will vote for the next Ross Perot, Jesse Ventura, or Ralph
Nader, although all of those third-party candidates drew disproportionately from the ranks of the young. But it does mean
that party organizers should worry: This is as much an indict-
ment of the parties as it is a comment about the voters.

My conversations with all but the most outwardly partisan
young people show a deep wariness of party identification and
almost a pride in maintaining one's independence. It's as if they
have absorbed the expectations of what Michael Schudson calls
the "informed citizen" and taken it to new heights. Schudson,
author of *The Good Citizen: A History of American Civic Life*,
coined the phrase to describe the twentieth-century ideal citizen: one who is informed about parties, persons and issues, who
places the public good above party loyalty, and who can choose
rationally among candidates regardless of party label.

Being an informed citizen is a time-consuming civic task. It
requires familiarizing oneself with lots of information about
the candidates' issues, platforms, and characters, and choosing
among them without the convenient screen of party preference
and loyalty. How much easier it is to pull the partisan lever. It's
why we root for baseball teams rather than individual players
and why we purchase a particular brand of ice cream rather than
constantly evaluate the price and taste of a freezer full of op-
tions. Choice can sometimes be a burden.

Independence, though, has its own rewards and attractions.
This generation abhors labels and exhibits a strong, libertarian
streak that helps explain its dislike of party identification.
Zachary Zitko, a twenty-nine-year-old business consultant and
organizer of young professionals who volunteer for community
projects, recently described himself and his generation in a
story published in the *Cincinnati Enquirer*. Young people shun
organized politics for the same reasons they shun organized

religion, he said—because they value independent thinking. "People don't want to be labeled," according to Zitko. "Once you label yourself as a Democrat or a Republican, all of a sudden all these other stereotypes come in. People assume that because you favor A and B, you also support C."

Over and over, I heard the same explanation from my students, even from political science majors in their senior year of college who rued their own sense of confusion about where they stood on the political spectrum. They know they need to situate themselves somewhere because that's the rule in a two-party republic, but neither choice is that appealing.

"We feel more comfortable in a nonpartisan activity. Even though I know that we eventually have to make a choice, I don't think that the parties will reflect our attitudes, " said Rachel Kreinces, a Penn junior from Long Island. "If you are a Republican, my mental image is that you are a gun-carrying racist who wants the rich to stay rich. If you are a Democrat, I think you are a liberal who wants to invest all the government's money in welfare programs. Whether these stereotypes are accurate is immaterial; they are powerful images that many of my friends share."

As Mark Mellman noted earlier, the young tend to be all over the map when it comes to ideology and issues, and their nuanced, often idiosyncratic views don't fit neatly into a preset party platform. Young people tend to be socially tolerant (pro gay rights, for instance) and yet have a strong conservative streak (the largest segment supporting the war with Iraq was eighteen- to thirty-year-olds). Compared with their elders, they tend to favor using tax money for school vouchers—a typically conservative approach to education reform—but they also favor stricter gun control laws, a view usually tagged as "liberal." Unlike their baby-boomer parents, they show increasing trust in the United States military, especially after the September 11 terrorist attacks, which would be a boon to the Republican Party, but they also are more likely to approve of gay marriage and affirmative action programs, attitudes usually associated with Democrats.

You can understand why the party pols, so intent on shoring up their natural bases and ensuring that predictable voters get to the polls, would see this unpredictable generation as a problem. Plenty of older Americans don't align themselves perfectly with party platforms either, but the pull to make a choice in the voting booth is more powerful when there is some template, some history to draw upon. Few young people have that. Few are growing up with photographs of John F. Kennedy—or Ronald Reagan, for that matter—hanging above their beds.

Indeed, it's not only the rigidity of the party platforms that alienates young people; it is the combative, confrontational style of politics that turns them off and away. Will Marshall, president of the Progressive Policy Institute—the moderate think tank for Democrats—is fond of saying that his generation was not "engaged, but enraged." Well, today younger people don't like to be enraged. Besides a few wild and woolly anti-globalization demonstrations, we don't see much anger on the street from them, and that is not only an expression of apathy or disengagement. These are people who grew up taking conflict resolution classes in school, who were admonished not to bully or name-call, who directed the crudeness of their culture into entertainment and music rather than political discourse. The rough-and-tumble of politics as it always was and likely always will be is simply not very appetizing to this younger generation.

As a result, even those inclined to be politically engaged sometimes turn away. Michael Schimmel decided to join the College Republicans when he arrived at the University of Pennsylvania, thinking it would be a good way to get involved in campus life. Then he started receiving e-mail messages from the GOP listserv, and was disgusted by the nasty tone, the insistent Democratic-bashing. "They were practically cursing," he said. Sadly, not only were his experiences corroborated by his classmates, but someone else had a similar story of attraction and repulsion to tell—about the College Democrats.

"Everything has become a black-and-white war of idealism," laments Nick Walters, a self-described political junkie who finds himself at sea on Penn's campus. "Most East Coast colleges have their College Democrats, who are extremely left wing, and College Republicans, who are a small, fringe group of boisterous iconoclasts. The result is a paradox of seemingly heightened interest when these two groups debate or battle each other, and a simultaneous alienation of many students who don't want to take sides or don't agree with the extremist views of both groups."

He goes on: "As a moderate, I often feel compelled by Democrats' social idealism and Republicans' fiscal responsibility. But I do not need to have the label of crazy, right-wing zealot by championing the CR [College Republicans] causes, nor do I need to support a lot of issues that I don't agree with simply to be in the College Democrats. The result is that the university has lost a very political, socially conscious student to the divisiveness and bureaucracy of the student political groups."

Young people feel ill served by the parties, and by one another. There's no galvanizing issue like the military draft to overcome the educational, economic, and geographic differences that have left young people without a unified voice. The special interests that exercise power over the party establishments don't want to hear from young, sometime-voters who challenge their stands on core issues—such as Democrats in favor of school vouchers, or Republicans who believe in gay rights. "The process keeps them away," Birch Bayh told me recently. "The establishment doesn't want them to rock the boat."

Unfortunately, the one chance to unify this generation politically was squandered. Even as the ruins of the Twin Towers still smoldered in Manhattan, the central message from our nation's leaders was that people should shop to help the economy. There was no call for joint sacrifice other than to expect longer lines at the security checkpoints in airports. Except for those young people who suffered a direct loss of a loved one, the September 11 attacks affected each of them differently, if at all. Unlike what *Newsweek* proclaimed, they did not become "Generation 9/11." As Sitaraman and Warren wrote in *Invisible Citizens*:

> *September 11 has affected our generation in the same way it has affected the rest of the nation, but it was not an event generated by or for us, and hence cannot serve as a statement of our purpose. The Vietnam War was fought and supported, resisted and protested by young people; they were definitively shaped by the event because they were directly involved in its progress. Similarly, World War II shaped the Greatest Generation. Thus far, the War on Terrorism has not engaged our generation; we are neither decision makers nor participants. As such, 9/11 does not constitute the defining moment for our generation; it, like MTV, is outside of our control.*

* * *

What September 11 did grant this generation, and indeed all Americans, was a momentary glimpse of a nation traumatized by attack but also strengthened by it. Anyone who lived through those awful hours and days remembers the palpable sense of patriotism and compassion that enveloped neighborhoods far, far away from the actual horror. The candlelight vigils and fund-raising drives did play to the central strengths of many young people, calling upon their innate ability to empathize and to reach out to help others in need.

But even the civic institutions involved in organizing and healing were careful to keep it all "above" politics, as if the political sphere had nothing to do with the nation's foreign policy and domestic security. The message was: Donate, spend, and travel. The message was *not* vote and participate, because that, and not our considerable wealth and military power, is what truly distinguishes us from our enemies. Much as we might blame political parties for actively neglecting the nation's newest citizens, we also have to expect more of the civic institutions—educational, religious, and communal—that interact with young people day in and day out.

Too many of these institutions have failed to show young people why it's important to vote and participate in civic life. Schools rarely encourage voter registration, the way Oceanside High did in 1972. How often do churches, synagogues, and mosques encourage their young congregants to become involved? How often do coaches require their players to register and vote? Why, half of this generation's parents don't even go to the polls. Beyond the absence of encouragement, there are also institutions that actively dissuade the young from getting involved politically. AmeriCorps members, for instance, are prohibited by law from engaging in any political activity, even something as benign as helping others register to vote.

We don't ask young people to get involved, and they respond in kind.

To change that, we have to start asking them. The best research on this subject, done by Donald P. Green and Alan S. Gerber, two political science professors at Yale University (along with David W. Nickerson, a doctoral candidate), has found that pre–Election Day face-to-face canvassing can increase youth turnout by 8 to 12 percent. That is a significant finding. Presidential elections have turned on less.

Civic institutions that touch the lives of young people— schools, churches, athletic teams, social clubs, stores, and coffee bars—must join the celebrity movie stars, wrestlers, and hip-hop artists in their campaign to increase citizen awareness and behavior. The power of the "personal ask" in politics can never be underestimated.

There's no better illustration of this central verity than Kris Hart, who is now a twenty-one-year-old junior at George Washington University and probably one of the most thoroughly politicized human beings I've ever met. Trim, intense, with a clipped speaking style and a professional manner, Hart sounds like a born political junkie when, in fact, politics was never discussed around the table in his childhood home. Instead, the active encouragement of a teacher and then a politician led him to where he is today: president of GWU's student body, second vice chairman and finance director of the College Republican National Committee. He had changed schools quite a bit in early adolescence, but by eighth grade had found a history teacher who recognized his interest in civics and politics. Learn more about Congress and government, she urged.

The next year, during summer vacation, Hart was bussing tables at Phil's Tavern in Ambler, Pennsylvania, a popular restaurant in the Philadelphia suburbs, and during quiet moments would chat with a waitress about his burgeoning interest. Just before his shift ended late one night—a Wednesday, he remembers—the waitress pointed out that a local congressman was seated at one of their tables. It was Jon Fox, an amiable, two-term Republican who was locked in a tight reelection bid in a district seesawing between the parties. Hart isn't sure what possessed him to approach the table and ask a few questions, but the next thing he knew, he was invited to eat with Fox and two campaign aides. Enthralled by the invitation and the conversation, Kris eagerly took up Fox's offer to volunteer with the campaign the very next day. He was so young, his father had to drive him to the congressional office.

One day with the campaign, and he was hooked. "I'd go to all the events after school and on Saturdays—hand out literature, go door-to-door," Hart recalled. Mostly, he hung with the congressman: "I was closely tied to him. He was my mentor."

That November brought a crushing defeat—Fox lost by a mere 83 votes—and Hart is even shown crying in a photograph taken on election night. But the heartbreak only served to strengthen his commitment, and he was determined to get to Washington, even though he was years away from graduating high school. Accepted as a congressional page when he turned sixteen, he moved to the capital, attended classes with the other pages from 6 A.M. to 9 A.M. every day, and worked the Republican side of the House of Representatives from nine until late in the day. "It was one of the coolest experiences ever," he says. After that year was over he got an appointment in the other half of the Capitol building, and became the youngest full-time paid employee in the U.S. Senate. Then, after earning a high school diploma, he still couldn't leave Washington and wound up studying at GWU.

Hart's story is hardly typical of his generation—or a typical story in any generation. Few people engaged in politics today can match Kris Hart's single-minded drive and willingness to become absorbed at such an early age. Bill Frist, the Senate majority leader, was a surgeon by training and didn't even register to vote until 1988. Wesley Clark, the decorated war commander, never thought about running for office until he decided to chase after the Democratic nomination for president in 2003. Congress, especially the Senate, is increasingly populated with successful businessmen who, after shoring up their financial portfolio, decide that it's time to do a little public service. Americans tend to be wary of those who have invested their lives in the political sphere, as if prolonged exposure to politics and government leads to a kind of parasitic social disease or an uncontrollable, unseemly quest for power.

Kris Hart's story may not be typical, but it is instructive. He wasn't born a Kennedy or a Bush; he didn't fall into the family business. At a time when so many people his age turn off or turn away, he was turned on by a couple of caring adults and a process that continues to delight and fascinate him. But he is also frustrated by his peers' laziness and apathy, and unwillingness to vote and get involved in issues that directly affect their lives. "If we started coming out to vote, we could say that the Medicare bill is way too big. I want to help the elderly, but you can't put me in debt," he argues.

And, despite his avowed Republicanism and position in the party's national collegiate organization, he is loath to wrap himself completely in a partisan flag. "I have conservative tendencies, but on some social issues I have liberal leanings. That's true of all youth," he says. "You just tie yourself down if you identify too much with a party."

Kris Hart is the embodiment of what can happen when a young person is asked to get involved. You listen to young people like him—and there are more around than you realize—and suddenly America's civic future doesn't seem so bleak. I first met Hart in Washington at an event called Democracy Day, on September 17, 2003, the anniversary of the signing of the U.S. Constitution; he was part of a panel discussion that I moderated. The participants were diverse racially, educationally, politically, but as articulate as Barbara Jordan and as inspiring as Winston Churchill. I fantasized on the train ride home to Philadelphia what the nation could be like with these young people in charge. It was a happy thought.

Someone—a parent, a teacher, a stranger at a restaurant—encouraged these young people to get involved. Sometimes an entire community mobilizes to transform young people into active citizens. That has happened in Chicago, where the turnout of young African Americans in certain elections is as high as 90 percent, propelled by the many organizations—Jesse Jackson's Rainbow/PUSH Coalition, citywide civic education programs, religious institutions—who teach, preach, cajole, and literally drive young people to the polls.

We'll never have a generation filled with Kris Harts; few people are addicted to living such a political life. But we can do more to create a generation that knows enough and cares enough to cast a vote, the simplest, most common act of citizenship and yet the thing we have let slip through our hands.

CHAPTER FIVE

The Service Gap:
Why so many young people think community service is more effective than voting— which is a shame, because it isn't

On the morning of January 20, 1997, I loaded my three school-age girls and a few of their friends into our van and headed for a dilapidated church in North Philadelphia for what was then a little-known project called the King Day of Service. We arrived at the appointed hour and were told to sit in a cavernous, second-floor space that needed a good scrub—and more—before it could be transformed into a drug and alcohol rehab center.

There, in a room filled with an array of chattering students and adults, we waited. And waited. Finally, an hour and a half later, we were given a rousing sermon and put to work. Only there weren't enough paintbrushes, or ladders, or rollers to paint the alcove. There weren't enough new squares of carpet to replace the worn ones. The older kids managed to keep occupied; my youngest daughter, seven years old at the time, felt useless. We left midday, half satisfied that we had made, perhaps, a small contribution to a needy neighborhood.

That evening, I asked my youngest daughter as I put her to bed, "Wouldn't it be great if next year all the kids in your grade volunteered on King Day?"

"But, Mom," she replied, "will there be something to do?"

This was months before the four living presidents gathered for a summit at Independence Hall in Philadelphia to boost volunteerism and launch the nationwide effort known as America's Promise. This was before community service became so fashionable and a graduation requirement in many high

72

schools, a virtual admissions requirement for top-notch colleges. Before AmeriCorps, City Year, and Teach for America became household names and before books like Robert Putnam's *Bowling Alone* became cocktail party chatter. The civic renewal movement, which argues that a breakdown in social capital in America has weakened communities and threatens democracy, was just gaining attention.

To answer my daughter's plaintive question, there is now more than enough to do on King Day. The holiday emerged from its birthing pains to become a well-organized, national effort which in 2004 drew 40,000 volunteers in the Philadelphia area alone. Young people, especially, are being drawn to service in record numbers, volunteering at rates higher than their elders and often venturing far from the safety and comforts of home. High schools kids are spending their summer vacations repairing homes on Indian reservations in Montana and building school lunchrooms in St. Lucia. Or tutoring kids in inner-city public schools. Or cleaning neighborhood parks and streams.

There are lots of statistics describing this trend. Here are just a few, drawn from the website of Youth Service America, a Washington-based organization founded in 1986 to serve as a resource center to increase the quality and quantity of volunteer opportunities for young people. The number of high school students involved in service learning increased nearly 4,000 percent during the 1990s. UCLA's annual college survey found that 82.6 percent of incoming freshman reported frequent or occasional volunteer work in 2001, compared to 81 percent the previous year and 66 percent in 1989. The Center for Democracy and Citizenship found in 2002 that 72 percent of young adults say they have donated money, clothes, or food to a community or church organization in the past couple of years.

To put this in a generational perspective, a study of the nation's civic and political health released in 2002 by CIRCLE, the Center for Information and Research on Civic Learning and Engagement, posited that 40 percent of fifteen to twenty-five-year-olds gave time to a group in the past year, compared to one-third of Generation Xers and boomers, and just 22 percent of those Americans born before 1946.

You get the idea.

The civic benefits for the volunteer and the recipients cannot be underestimated. Service pushes teenagers, the most self-centered of human beings, out into the world, opening their eyes and ears, and with hope their hearts and minds, to the conditions of others. And if the service work is tailored to the needs of a community, it can be absolutely essential. Government is simply never going to take care of all social needs, and the truth is, sometimes the congregants from a local church or the strapping youngsters in a summer service program are more effective.

Besides, volunteering is often gratifying in a way that voting and politics will never be. For a generation grown accustomed to the immediacy of microwave cooking and instant messaging, the ability to see the fruits of their labor firsthand and quickly has enormous appeal. They feel good inside when the stream looks that much cleaner or the third grader finally can read a chapter on his own.

"Community service is dignified," says Kris Hart, the George Washington University student leader, neatly summing up the sentiment of his peers.

For many young people, service is becoming the new politics, a training ground for leadership, a channel for a great deal of youthful energy and idealism, and—here's the worrisome part—a substitute for the accumulation and exercise of political power. A survey conducted by Harvard's Institute of Politics in 2000 found that 85 percent of college students feel that volunteerism is better than political engagement for addressing issues facing the community. On this issue, the generation gap again is apparent: Just 3 percent of young adults say they volunteered for a political group in the past year, the lowest rate for any segment of the population studied by CIRCLE. And in that survey, only 10 percent of young people cited their volunteer work as a means to address a political or social problem, compared to, say, 26 percent of their boomer parents.

Instead, for increasing numbers of young people, service is framed either as an individualistic act of compassion (such as tutoring) or a consumer behavior, in which writing a check for a charity or boycotting certain products becomes the preferred method of civic involvement. With this perspective, not only does voting take a backseat, but it sits there with other traditional forms of engagement—writing a letter to a public official, reading a newspaper, marching in protest against something. Often, this isn't a rejection of or a substitution for the ballot box alone, but reflects a larger disconnect from government itself. A new kind of citizen is emerging, and the prospect is troubling.

This wasn't supposed to happen. When the service movement began gathering steam a decade ago, the hope was that it would provide young people a back door into political engagement by broadening their communal experiences, creating a shared sense of national identity, and encouraging them to develop their own perspectives on how government can solve larger social problems. This was not wishful thinking. Just as we expect military service to strengthen national pride and enhance an understanding of the world beyond these shores, community service can perform similar functions back at home. The nation has depended on its rich network of voluntary associations to strengthen its civic and political life even before Alexis de Tocqueville observed as much in his famous assessment of American democracy in the 1830s.

Nowadays, however, instead of a back door to a larger world, the service gap is becoming a trapdoor, an insidious either/or choice when in fact maintaining a healthy constitutional democracy relies on citizens involved in *both* the voluntary *and* political spheres. Even those in the service movement are awakening to this sobering reality. "Service as politics is incredibly dangerous," warns Steven A. Culbertson, president and CEO of Youth Service America. "I tell the young people I work with that if you volunteer but don't vote, twenty years from now your kids are going to be cleaning the same dirty rivers and tutoring in the same lousy schools."

To return to the question my daughter posed at that early King Day event—Will there be something to do?—the answer is: Don't worry. If present trends continue, there will still be plenty for volunteers to do.

* * *

The current infatuation with community service is, like so many other social behaviors in contemporary America, subject to the caveat of class. Young people who do not attend college— that is, roughly half the eighteen- to twenty-five-year-olds in America—are less likely to vote, to be registered to vote, or to feel they can make a difference in their communities when compared to their peers in college, according to yet another study compiled by CIRCLE, this one in 2003. Those without college experience are also more likely to view voting as a right or a choice rather than a responsibility or a duty. They don't talk politics with their parents as frequently and—no matter what some might say about the liberal, antiestablishment biases on college campuses—it is the student who isn't in college who tends to be more mistrustful of government.

So it should come as no surprise that the levels of volunteering in the non-college crowd are markedly lower. Drawing from a 2002 youth survey, CIRCLE found that 28 percent of college students reported that they had never volunteered, compared to 48 percent of the non-college students.

This discrepancy can partly be explained by logic—many of the young people not partaking of higher education may not have the luxury of donating their time, and some may even be the sort of people community service is designed to help. Besides, there's a dirty little secret about some of the service models now prevalent at Ivy League universities and top-notch high schools: Service can be expensive. Summer programs offering the chance to volunteer in California or Costa Rica come with a hefty price tag, sometimes costing several thousand dollars. Other opportunities close to home can be off-limits to less affluent students who must work while they are in school or during vacations, or who must earn more than the modest stipend offered by such AmeriCorps programs as City Year and Teach for America. A friend of mine confided that she'd really like her teenage daughter to do a volunteer program in the summer, rather than work at a local day camp. "But," she said ruefully, "we can't afford it."

Perhaps this explains one of the few things that college students and those not in college agree on: A sizable majority in each group are in favor of offering young people the chance to do community service in exchange for money to pay for education. Not everyone can contribute to their community for free.

* * *

Besides being driven by class, the service movement is also grappling with another holdover social issue: gender. Even for the most egalitarian generation that America has ever seen, stubborn stereotypes persist and, in many ways, volunteer work largely remains women's work.

Dan Koken, a student in my class at the University of Pennsylvania, encountered this gender gap in an unexpected place.

An athletic senior from Colorado, he's your basic guy's guy—captain of his high school wrestling team, starting player on Penn's rugby team, president of his fraternity. He also enjoys helping disadvantaged children, so he's tutored underprivileged kids in Philadelphia and volunteered in a middle school in Camden, New Jersey. His volunteer work last summer in an orphanage for abused and abandoned children in Guatemala was a natural extension of his interest. But one aspect of the experience surprised him: There were hardly any other men. Only two others, to be exact, in a group of seventeen.

When Koken raised this point during class one day, heads all around the large conference table nodded in agreement. Another student, Rachel Kreinces, coordinates a program called Write On, in which Penn students coach public school students in writing skills, and she confessed to having a devilish time attracting male volunteers to the program. Likewise, many of the popular summer programs that send students to impoverished communities to build schools and homes—hardly easy work—are predominantly filled with young women. Even well-established national programs are witnessing a gender gap in enrollment. For instance, City Year corps members, who devote a year to serving gritty urban neighborhoods, are 58 percent female, 42 percent male. "We'd like it to be fifty-fifty, but we're not there yet," says Alan Khazei, City Year cofounder and chief executive officer. "A lot of the work we do is human service work, and these professions historically have attracted women more than men."

The gender gap goes beyond human service work, however. You'd think that volunteering for an organization like Habitat for Humanity would be particularly attractive to men accustomed to using hammer and nail, but you would be wrong. A survey of students at four-year colleges done by Peter D. Hart Research Associates in May 2002 found that significantly more women were interested in working with Habitat than men. (The number was 53 percent versus 36 percent.)

Sure, there are the exceptions, the guys who coach basketball teams and organize soccer leagues, or play with sick kids at the Ronald McDonald House, as Koken has done. But the gender gap is noticeable enough in the service community that the Corporation for National Service (CNS) has published a guide for organizations seeking to recruit more male volunteers. The guide's author, Stephanie T. Blackman, opens her lengthy work by recalling a poster of a muscular woman lifting weights with a text reading, "Macho is not a gender thing." Neither, she thought, is volunteerism. "And yet," she writes, "when it comes to social service, female volunteers seem to be the norm, suggesting that perhaps volunteering *is* a 'gender thing.'"

The service community is starting to take notice. "Traditionally, service has been more appealing and appropriate for women, and I don't think we've outgrown that yet," says Steven A. Culbertson, president and CEO of Youth Service America. "Service is a nurturing idea—feeding, clothing, teaching. We've got to make these programs more user-friendly to guys, to appeal more to men's egos and skills." Indeed, the CNS guide to recruiting men notes just these obstacles: Many men must be convinced to overcome "the breadwinner syndrome," which approves of work only if it is paid. They need to be seen as "nurturers" and need positive reinforcement for their efforts, and that, too, is not often found in volunteering with society's downtrodden.

For his part, Dan Koken says that he's received nothing but praise for his volunteer efforts. He thinks he's avoided ridicule because of his "traditionally macho activities and characteristics" and that more men like him need to be included in the public face of service to counter the impression that it is mostly women's work. The CNS guide also made that recommendation, suggesting that billboards, advertisements, public service announcements and posters depict positive images of male volunteers (not unlike the poster image of a woman lifting weights). The gender gap eventually will narrow even more, I believe, as more schools mandate service learning in the classroom and more school districts require a certain number of hours of community service for graduation. Once girls and boys, young men and women, are asked to fulfill the same expectations regardless of gender, we can reasonably hope that tutoring a child will be no more women's work than coaching Little League is considered a man's job.

* * *

Despite the drawbacks of class and gender, the attraction of service for young people is undeniable, and growing. It is propelled by the characteristics of this generation—their tendency toward compassion and their nonjudgmental concern for others, and away from what they see as a political system driven by conflict and ego. But we cannot overlook the fact that those tendencies are reinforced by people in power at the highest levels. I'm not simply referring to school officials who institute community service requirements, or college admissions counselors who all but require such work, or even goodhearted parents, clergy, and coaches who urge young people to give of themselves. I'm talking about the greatest bully pulpit in the world— the U.S. presidency.

Beginning with George H. W. Bush's idea of the Points of Light Foundation, followed by Bill Clinton's creation of AmeriCorps and his constant cheerleading on behalf of community service, and continuing with George W. Bush's passionate call for Americans to volunteer, the presidency has served this issue well. One can debate whether policies have matched rhetoric— particularly in the recent case of AmeriCorps funding—but the rhetoric itself is without blemish or qualification. This is the only issue that drew all the presidents, past and current, together, at the 1997 Philadelphia summit to promote volunteerism and service. This was the focus of President Bush's admonitions after the September 11 terrorist attacks, when he said, "The best way to fight evil is by doing good," and thereafter created the USA Freedom Corps, an umbrella agency coordinating efforts for those Americans who are willing and able to give two years of service to their community and country over the course of a lifetime. Presidential awards for service are given out regularly, scholarships are offered, and signing up for volunteer opportunities large and small is available with the click of a mouse. Whether each and every young adult is aware of these details is debatable, but there's no doubt that the message is getting through loud and clear.

By contrast, you don't hear the president urging young people to vote, or read a newspaper, or write to their state representatives. You don't see the White House or governor's mansion hosting award ceremonies for those who registered a record number of new voters. And you surely don't see a political system eager to make it as easy to vote as it is to sign up for Saturday's park cleanup.

"We've done a very good job of building up service and service learning, whereas our political system is less welcoming," notes Culbertson of Youth Service America. "Politics gives out only negative messages, while there's nothing but positive messages about service. That kind of reinforcement feels very good. We've created a user-friendly infrastructure for service, but not for politics. Politics to young people seems like a dizzying array of acrimony and inaccessibility, whereas service gives them immediate feedback and results."

This is not an accident. When community service became nationalized and codified, it did so only by becoming avowedly apolitical. Those who worked on the tortuous path toward congressional approval of AmeriCorps recall that the only way to get the bill past skeptical and, in some cases, hostile Republicans was to strip the program of any and all political involvement. Some of this is highly understandable—after all, we don't want taxpayer money funding voter registration drives that could be perceived to help one party or candidate over others (especially if, as many in the GOP feared, such drives in poor communities would boost Democratic rolls). But it has been taken to extremes. City Year, whose goal is not only to provide a venue for meaningful service but to improve democracy, used to insist that all its corps members were registered to vote, and asked them to show proof. Until, that is, the organization was reminded of the fine print in the AmeriCorps regulations, which allows City Year to *encourage* eligible members to register and vote, but can't require it. Coming from the nation's premier service entity, the message is clear: Service is great. Voting is optional.

That service by itself heightens political and civic awareness is undeniable. Robert Putnam, a leading scholar in dissecting the whys and wherefores of American social capital, says that young people who volunteer are more likely to vote, an observation born out by the experience of City Year alumni. A few years ago, City Year surveyed alumni to find out who voted in the 1996 presidential election and calculated the results based on the age and education levels of corps members. The story was heartening: City Year alums voted at a rate between 26 and 39 percent higher than other registered voters of similar age and educational attainment, and the impact was greatest among those who, because of their background, were least likely to vote. Fifty-nine percent of the corps members who had only a high school diploma voted, compared to 23 percent in the overall population; 53 percent of those who hadn't yet graduated went to the polls, compared to a general turnout rate of 14 percent.

"We've seen the impact. When people get engaged in the community, they are turned on to participate," says Alan Khazei, City Year's cofounder. Still, even those working knee-deep in the fertile field of service like Culbertson and Khazei are worried that the message is not getting through to enough of the young people participating in their programs. Outside of yearlong commitments like City Year and Teach for America, the bulk of young people volunteer sporadically, for a semester, a fortnight, or even for a day here and there. Mark Lopez's work at CIRCLE has confirmed that the rise in volunteering by young people is driven mostly by an increase in episodic rather than regular activity (episodic volunteers are those who do so once a month or less). He's also found that most of this volunteer work is directed toward youth organizations, civic or community groups, and environmental concerns, and not for political organizations or candidates.

The trend toward episodic volunteering runs the risk of being overtaken by cynicism. Consider what Elizabeth Powers, a sophomore at Radnor High School outside Philadelphia, wrote in a class assignment later published in the *Inquirer*:

I enjoyed doing community service—until I went to high school. I still think service is rewarding and one of the best ways I can spend my free time, but I've grown to resent all the things that go along with it. Volunteering is a wonderful thing when the volunteers have a desire to help their community or make a difference, but now it seems that every kid is joining a service club, not because he or she is interested, but because college admissions boards like that sort of thing. Spending my Saturday de-littering a park sounds like a great idea until I hear: "It looks great on your college application."

* * *

Young people are also beginning to realize that the paths of volunteering and voting are diverging dramatically, and may end up leaving their generation with political muscles that have atrophied and political bases that never had a chance to build clout. Community service will never be able to craft policy, establish regulations, and enact laws that affect more than a single school or park; even at its best, it is no more than a temporary fix within eyesight, not able to address the larger problems that we cannot or will not see. Ann Ochsendorf, in a recent letter to the *New York Times,* said it eloquently:

Many of us who were in college in the 1990s also believed we could change the world through direct service. Now, after spending a few years teaching in schools crippled by lack of funds, building youth development programs that have since been dismantled by the Bush administration and realizing that no amount of "socially responsible" buying will counteract the harmful effects of weakened environmental legislation, we've learned that there is no substitute for active involvement in the political system. I hope that students will begin to put as much energy into politics as they do into community service.

This isn't just a complaint from the political left. Kris Hart, the president of GWU's student body and a proud College Republican, laments that his fellow students would rather volunteer for a day than lobby Congress for legislation to reduce what he contends are the crippling costs of college tuition.

Erin Ross experienced similar frustration, shared it with friends at Tufts University, and channeled it into creating United Leaders, a small, spunky, innovative organization with nothing less than national aspirations to bridge the "service gap" among her peers. There was no "service gap" in Ross's childhood growing up in Colorado and California; her parents were committed to both service and politics, bringing their children to ladle food in soup kitchens on holidays and cheering for candidates at political rallies. In high school, she was one of the "*über* servers"—over a hundred hours of volunteering a year for seven years, she recalls—but she never made the connection between service and politics until one unforgettable encounter with political reality. One of her most satisfying volunteer gigs was helping out in a home for children who had been taken from their own abused situations—until California's budget cuts forced the center to close. "It made me realize that all the service I was doing had to be about something bigger," she says. "We don't want to create a culture of service that gives and gives and gives and never makes any change."

So Ross and a few college friends involved in student government decided to create an organization that would give young people the tools, the networks and the inspiration to "move from the soup kitchen to the Senate." Now headquartered in Boston, with an office in Washington that Ross directs, United Leaders offers programs for high school and college students as well as an intensive summer experience to awaken the consciousness of their peers. It's an uphill climb, but they are finding a receptive audience.

"My generation's commitment to service is great, but in the end it doesn't solve anything," says Ross, now an articulate twenty-three-year-old. "We have grown up in a time of individualism. We're content to do things on our own, and we want the praise for doing things on our own. We cut our political teeth on the [Clinton] impeachment hearings, when both sides of the aisle behaved abysmally. I can't blame people who don't want to be part of this political system. But the service gap isn't getting anything done."

So United Leaders will organize a day of service where students will help clean up a blighted neighborhood—and then will meet with a city council member to discuss the challenge of creating more affordable housing in urban communities. It runs a program called "Politics for Dummies," to counteract the sense on many college campuses that politics is only a blood sport and government an intimidating bureaucracy of questionable value. "We're trying to create a nonpartisan place for discussion of ideas rather than partisan policy," Ross says. "Students don't feel comfortable talking about politics because they are afraid they don't know it all. And we're also trying to bridge the reverse service gap—some students are so interested in politics that they have lost touch with the community. We're trying to bring the two groups together."

It's anybody's guess whether these efforts can make a dent in helping young people understand the connections between community needs, policy solutions, and the exercise of political power. The news is peppered daily with examples of the raw display of lobbying muscle in Congress, whether from the energy industry or pharmaceutical companies, and the more subtle threats to political survival issued by those who know how to deliver votes on Election Day. Rarely are the issues directly facing young people now, or in the future, included in this mix. The explosive growth of a federal budget deficit that will hang around the necks of our children and grandchildren for decades is but one glaring example. Meantime, there should be a real concern that the Band-Aid, stopgap measures offered by episodic community service will relieve government—and by extension, the public—of the responsibility to feed the hungry, protect the environment, and school the next generation. Relying on government to care for all social needs is, of course, a foolhardy strategy in twenty-first-century America. But relying on the voluntary sector—with its well-meaning but often undependable and untrained workforce—to complete these essential tasks alone is similarly unrealistic and even dangerous.

The day before the famous Presidents' Summit in Philadelphia in 1997, a massive cleanup of Germantown Avenue, a central but seedy thoroughfare, was organized with great fanfare and media attention. More than 6,000 people volunteered to work alongside former presidents and future secretaries of state to scrub, paint, and beautify crumbling storefronts and row house walls. After the television cameras and Secret Service agents left, however, Germantown Avenue was improved, but not by much, for this simple reason: Volunteer work is inherently inefficient. Much of the cleanup and refurbishing was better completed by paid, trained staff who knew how to properly coat the wall of an aging building and strip graffiti from high above the street. As a galvanizing effort to bring together the community, it was a splendid success. (And as a political photo op, it was brilliant.) But let's not forget that the cleanup was meant first to help the Germantown Avenue neighborhood, not those who came from afar to temporarily hoist a paintbrush.

* * *

No example better illustrates the danger of believing that service can substitute for political power than the story of the AmeriCorps funding crisis in 2003. It is living proof that no amount of do-gooding can replace the cold, hard fact that bills are passed and money is doled out by government, and that sometimes only the exercise of raw, brute political muscle can hold politicians accountable for their promises.

Devotees of national service are quick to point out that theirs is not a new idea, nor did it begin as a partisan one. In an essay written in 1910, William James suggested that nonmilitary contribution to the health of the nation should be considered "the moral equivalent of war." Presidents Kennedy, Johnson, and the first Bush all attempted to institutionalize this patriotic impulse, whether in the Peace Corps, Volunteers in Service to America (VISTA), or the Points of Light Foundation. That is not to say the programs were welcomed universally—some Republicans derided the Peace Corps as the "Kiddie Korps," while some Democrats ridiculed the Points of Light as nothing more than red, white, and blue window dressing. But the programs were benign enough in outlook and modest enough in size to keep a patriotic, and not partisan, aura about them.

That is, until 1988, when then-Governor Bill Clinton embraced the Democratic Leadership Council's proposal to condition federal college student aid on a broadened national service program. The innovative idea became one of his best applause lines in the 1992 presidential campaign, and the establishment of a national service corps in 1993 one of the first major accomplishments of his presidency. Clinton's deep identification with AmeriCorps was a blessing and a curse; it meant that the president's famously relentless cheerleading could always be dispatched to keep the flame alive, but it also meant that many Republicans would fiercely oppose the concept for no other reason than that it was his.

AmeriCorps was established as a new kind of federal/local, public/private partnership. While the agency in Washington distributes funding and coordinates some activities, much of the action takes place on the state and local level. States decide where a chunk of funding is spent, while local community groups, national nonprofits, and faith-based organizations are invited to bid on direct grants. And though anyone from seventeen to eighty may apply for AmeriCorps, the program mostly attracts young people who want to devote a year or two to national service and receive a modest stipend of $9,600 and the promise of a $4,725 educational grant in return.

Funding crises have dogged AmeriCorps since its inception, but nothing was quite like 2003, a year when the agency was supposed to pay for 67,000 corps members to tutor in schools, clean blighted neighborhoods, and replenish the environment. In fact, the number shrunk as the year wore on. Trouble was foreshadowed at the end of 2002, when the Corporation for National and Community Service, which oversees AmeriCorps and other federal service initiatives, instituted what it euphemistically called a "pause" in hiring—in truth, a hiring freeze. The CNCS was afraid that the education trust, which distributes the $4,725 grants to each corps member who completes a year of service, was running out of money. The freeze was lifted in March of 2003, after Congress allocated an additional $100 million, but the damage was done. Programs nationwide were left hanging, lawmakers were fuming, and the odor of mismanagement began to infect this small but always vulnerable agency.

Then comes a story of government at its sorriest. Annoyed members of Congress insisted that the 22,000 slots already in the pipeline during the hiring freeze should be counted against a 50,000 cap they had put in place for fiscal 2003. That left 28,000 openings. But then the General Accounting Office decided that AmeriCorps officials had grossly underfunded the education trust, and it demanded that the difference be made up immediately. Although the Office of Management and Budget disagreed, the GAO opinion took precedence. So 15,000 more slots were subtracted from the year's cap. By mid-June of 2003, word started to seep from Washington that the agency had only 13,000 slots to go to programs such as City Year, or as grants to states, VISTA, and countless smaller endeavors.

I first heard the news before it became public, from a prominent local businessman who was afraid that his beloved City Year would be decimated by these cuts. It was; Philadelphia's numbers were dramatically reduced, and some City Year programs were eliminated from the federal funding stream altogether. "Right now we're standing on the edge of the cliff,"

Martin Friedman, executive director of the National School and Community Corps, another AmeriCorps agency, told me at the time. "You want to know the impact? How about eight thousand Philadelphia students in the lowest-performing schools not having NSCC members to tutor and mentor them."

The stories of broken promises kept rolling in, and they were heartbreaking. Not all involved young people—I remember talking to an older woman, a self-described conservative Republican, who was beside herself because the AmeriCorps program she ran that offered respite to the caregivers of Alzheimer's patients in Florida was about to be cut. But most of the agencies suffering from the budget cuts were those who employed and served younger people, and the disillusionment this caused was profound. Consider, for instance, the impact of eliminating the education grant that had been promised to participants in Teach for America (TFA), a sterling program that trains bright college graduates to teach in the nation's neediest schools for two years. The grant, remember, was a mere $4,725 a year—which doesn't even pay for summer camp in some affluent communities—and it had not been increased in the ten years of AmeriCorps' existence. Still, Hong Mei Li, a twenty-two-year-old Philadelphian already accepted into a doctoral program, was counting on the money to help pay for graduate school and the continuing education courses she was required to take during her TFA experience. Here a young woman whose family had immigrated from China, who was forgoing her own education to give back to others, who was breathing life into the American dream, was being squeezed by a government unwilling to come up with a few thousand dollars.

There were more stories. I talked to Rick Schosield, twenty, whose juvenile parole officer referred him to an AmeriCorps program in Ohio where he was working in a state park and straightening out his life. "I wanted to be the first one in the family to go to college," he told me. "Now I found out they no longer have the education award. It's kind of like being cheated." And I spoke with Beth Boucher, twenty-two, a new City Year corps member in New Hampshire who was hoping the education award would help her pay off more than $20,000 in college loans. "We aren't rich people. We're willing to volunteer our time. And now this small amount of money is being held from us," she said ruefully.

As I scrambled to understand the impact across the nation and put it into human terms for the readers of my column, I realized that nothing I had covered in two decades of journalism had made me angrier. This was a program that was lauded in *two* State of the Union addresses by George W. Bush, who first became an AmeriCorps supporter while governor of Texas and now was a president eager to display the face of compassionate conservatism. This was a program that had proven itself to skeptics such as Pennsylvania's GOP senator Rick Santorum, who once famously derided it as a waste of money for a bunch of kids to "stand around a campfire holding hands and singing 'Kumbaya'" and now was one of its biggest champions. This was a program with a payback to the nation that was well documented and beneficial, even in purely economic terms: A cost-benefit analysis by the GAO estimated that AmeriCorps returns $1.60 to $2.60 for every dollar it spends. And it was a program whose biggest administrative sin was to try to accommodate the surge of Americans, mostly young people, who sought to answer the president's call for service in the wake of September 11. The alleged "mismanagement" involved no fraud, no embezzlement, no misleading statements on nuclear weapons, no loss of life or limb—just a bureaucratic failure to manage an outpouring of patriotism.

Yet this was a program on the verge of extinction, because its members and supporters did not seem to have the political clout to keep it alive. Years of operating in a strictly nonpartisan environment had left AmeriCorps weak and neutered; its emphasis on apolitical service and its decentralized structure meant that its core constituency was scattered and unorganized. The communities it served were hardly the special interest groups with the fanciest offices on K Street in Washington. It appeared that the Republicans gunning for AmeriCorps ever since it was a gleam in Bill Clinton's eye and the Democrats who were all too willing to criticize anything in the Bush administration would get away with this stunt with relative impunity. There was little political cost to be paid in harming a program that enlisted the young to serve the needy.

But like a stunned fighter who reels from the first blow and lunges back into the ring, the supporters of AmeriCorps shook off their shock and responded. By the first week of September 2003, they organized a round-the-clock vigil with speakers from all over the nation offering one hundred hours of testimony on Capitol Hill. More than 200 CEOs, 135 mayors, 1,200 community organizations, scores of governors, and too many newspaper editorials to count all expressed support for the program. A website (www.saveamericorps.org) was established to spread information and create a network of sympathizers.

The outpouring heightened AmeriCorps' profile immensely, but the actual results were mixed. The 2003 funding was never restored, and programs across the country had to close or shrink substantially, causing irreparable damage to their long-term efforts in communities. The outlook for fiscal 2004 turned brighter, however, when Congress approved a funding increase that should support a record 75,000 AmeriCorps members. "But for the outpouring across the country, this would have been a permanent cut," believes Alan Khazei of City Year. "This proved beyond a doubt that politics matter."

It certainly has changed City Year's perspective. The Boston-based organization with chapters in fourteen cities is rolling out a civics curriculum designed to close the "service gap" experienced by its members. The experience has strengthened Khazei's resolve to see national service expanded dramatically—not only to help communities in need but actually to change the nature of political debate and respond to the well-founded criticism of young people that politics is dominated by the extremes.

"Generally the extremes aren't right," Khazei says. "If you have a critical mass of national service participants, they're going to see problems from a citizen's point of view, because they've witnessed them firsthand. They have credibility, they won't be just another voice in the room. By getting more citizens engaged this way, we can actually lower the partisan dialogue."

That's the theory, anyway. Inspiring though it is, it requires bringing programs like AmeriCorps to scale, and that in turn requires the kind of consistent political will that has been missing all these years, the kind that Jennings Randolph embodied half a century ago. Today, a majority of young Americans favor receiving college tuition assistance in return for a year of service, and there's always a piece of legislation or two making just such a proposal. Without committed leadership backed up by strength at the polls, however, the legislation languishes and the idea will continue to remain in the recesses of the national agenda. Politics does matter. AmeriCorps supporters learned that the hard way.

* * *

When author and scholar Benjamin Barber was directing a program at Rutgers University years ago, he told me with some despair of a student who, after a year volunteering in a homeless shelter, said, "This was the most extraordinary experience I've ever had. I just hope my children will have a chance to do it."

Community service should not be constructed to perpetuate itself. It is a concrete act, but also a consciousness raiser that should lead the citizen to more knowledgeably assess which policies ought to be enacted to solve the larger problems of society. Students who tutor in underprivileged schools should be asked to reflect on the range of solutions out there to deal with education in distressed communities. Should funding be increased? School governance be reformed? Should vouchers be instituted? The conversation is about ideas and choice, not about partisanship. We have to reclaim the fine art of teaching about government without reverting to preaching about politics. This cannot happen by remaining enthralled with the romance of service without putting it into broader political context. As James L. Perry and Ann Marie Thompson note in their book, *Civic Service: What Difference Does It Make?*: "We have turned to civic service in extraordinary times to produce extraordinary results. By the same token, as a country, we have been unable to leverage our regard for civic service as a means for restoring civic obligation on a large scale." That can only happen, they argue, when we reinvigorate our political institutions and restore their integrity.

And it can only happen if we raise a generation that understands the democracy they inherit.

CHAPTER SIX

"Hating Politics Is Cool":
Why young people know so little about government, and why that matters

David Skaggs, the former Colorado congressman who is now executive director of the Center for Democracy and Citizenship, is a bow-tied, buttoned-down old hand working in a field of young people—trying, that is, to persuade them to vote and pay attention to politics. He has a wry sense of humor. He has to. He seems to take impish delight in asking this question: What's the difference between voting and recycling?

Neither voting nor recycling actually makes sense to a rational human being. Is one aluminum can tossed in a plastic bin going to make a noticeable difference to the environment? Is one vote? "Then," he asks rhetorically, "why is recycling up and voting down in this age group?"

Recycling, he answers, has been made easier and cheaper. Voting is neither easy nor, if time and effort is money, is it cheap. Recycling is pervasive, infiltrating schools, billboards, commercial products, streetscapes, even kitchen design. Voting is episodic, ignored, or derided.

"More important," Skaggs explains to me as we talk one summer morning in his polished Washington office, "there is faith. The environmental movement has been tremendously effective in instilling this faith. The civic engagement movement has not. Politics looks smarmy. Environmentalism looks nifty. That's the difference."

Somehow we've learned to talk about environmentalism to kindergartners, but we can't talk about citizenship to high school seniors. From the time they can watch *Sesame Street*, children learn not to "leave the water on when you brush your teeth"; by the time they are in high school, students say they feel almost guilty if they should mistakenly drop a plastic bottle in an unmarked trash receptacle. The recycling message is that embedded in their socialization.

Civics and government is instead often viewed through the lens of a consumer transaction, not a participatory activity. "There's no sense of civic-mindedness conveyed to young people, we've reduced it to a commercial metric rather than a commonwealth, as if there's no difference between government and Wal-Mart," Skaggs says. "It's all about, am I getting my money's worth out of government? And that contributes to grumpiness because if you're always looking for your money's worth, you're always going to be unhappy."

Skaggs is one of a growing number of activists who are concerned about the trends away from voting and political participation and are looking for answers in civic education. No, not the kind parents and grandparents remember with a grimace and a groan, in which reams of seemingly boring facts and figures wrapped in the American flag were tossed at disinterested students in the name of God and country and graduation requirements. How many senators does it take to override a presidential veto? How often are congressional districts redrawn? What does a Registrar of Wills do anyway? Unless you were planning a run for the White House, these bits of data were likely as useful as a slide rule is today for a student studying multivariable calculus. Only the rare, innovative teacher would have linked the dry facts to controversial and important news events. Too many civics courses received the bad rap they deserved.

Information is good; concepts and skills are better. I'm glad, as a working journalist, that I remember it takes two-thirds of those present in Congress to override a president's veto, and that districts are redrawn every ten years based on data from the U.S. Census (although that hasn't stopped power-grabbing politicians from attempting to do it more frequently). After all these years covering Philadelphia government, I still don't know what the Registrar of Wills does or why our tax money pays for his salary and office.

Knowing these random facts doesn't necessarily make me a better citizen, but a certain degree of knowledge does help, and too many of our young people are receiving precious little. A major report issued in February 2003 by CIRCLE and the Carnegie Foundation, entitled "The Civic Mission of Schools," detailed the appalling way civic education and the development of civic skills have fallen off the radar screen in too many American secondary schools. They found, for instance, that most formal civic education today consists of a single-semester course on government, compared to as many as three courses on democracy, civics, and government which were common until the 1960s.

The decline in civic education is the elephant in the room when we talk about why young people know so little about government and care even less. The lack of basic appreciation for what government can and cannot do frustrates even those who know otherwise. "Hating politics is cool," says Kris Hart, George Washington University's student body president, "cooler than liking politics." Student government is such a big deal at GWU that Hart has an office and a business card; still, he can't seem to get his friends to show up at rallies, study the issues, or care.

Considering the age of these kids, it's no wonder. They began to walk and talk when Ronald Reagan was president and the era of big government was declared over. They came of age during Bill Clinton's time, when the Oval Office became a late-night TV joke and faith in the political system took more blows than a prizefighter on a very bad day. As Ben Smilowitz, a firebrand student activist who now works for an organization called Youth Venture, says with a heavy dose of sarcasm, "Our generation grew up hearing that government is bad, so the first thing we're going to do is go out and vote, right?"

* * *

Chastising young people for their ignorance is hardly a winning strategy, although we tend to do it with great regularity, partly because there's so much supporting evidence. More young Americans know the name of the reigning American Idol and the city where the cartoon Simpsons live than know the political party of their state's governor, bemoaned the National Conference of State Legislatures (NCSL) in September 2002.

The horror-story statistics came from a national Internet survey conducted for the NCSL that found fifteen- to twenty-six-year-olds don't understand the ideals of citizenship, are disengaged from the political process, lack the knowledge necessary for self-government, and have a limited appreciation of American democracy. For instance, 66 percent of those surveyed "believe it's necessary to vote in order to be a good citizen," compared with 83 percent of Americans over age twenty-six. Forty percent of the younger respondents knew which party controlled Congress, compared to 61 percent of the older crowd.

Over the last few years, other surveys have found similarly depressing results. More teens can name the Three Stooges than the three branches of government. They know who founded Microsoft but not who fathered the Constitution. They think that Springfield is home to Bart Simpson, not Abraham Lincoln. More seriously, in the last national assessment test in history, only 18 percent of fourth graders, 17 percent of eighth graders, and 11 percent of high school seniors demonstrated what is loosely termed "proficiency." On the National Assessment of Educational Progress (NAEP) administered in 1998, only 9 percent of seniors could list two ways a democratic society can benefit if citizens take part.

As an antidote to this dire news, consider this: Political participation and knowledge affect each other reciprocally—increases in one will lead to increases in another. The same NCSL survey that catalogued youth ignorance and disengagement found that a little knowledge can go a long way in a positive direction. Young people who have taken a civics course are two to three times more likely to vote, follow government news, and contact a public official about an issue that concerns them. For instance, 71 percent of teens or young adults who have taken a government course believe voting is a necessary component of good citizenship, compared with 57 percent who didn't take such a course.

It's always dangerous to extrapolate too much from snapshot surveys of human behavior, but it stands to reason that exposure to the workings of government and the concepts of citizenship would positively influence a young person's perspective. Especially if we probe deeper into the attitudes of young people toward government. They may hate politics, for all the reasons discussed earlier, but that animus is not directed toward government per se. Instead of hostility, there is a profound disconnect, propelled by a belief that government simply is not relevant to their lives.

"Students don't know what to make of government," Peter D. Hart Research Associates wrote in an April 2001 report to the Penatta Institute in California. "Today's students are simultaneously progressive and apolitical; they embrace many government solutions, but evince little interest in government itself."

To test this theory, ask any young person whether, when they think about Congress, the state legislature, or City Hall, they say *the* government or *our* government. The Hart survey found that 60 percent used the preposition *the*, while only 39 percent used *our*. Based on my conversations with political science majors, I'm surprised the proportion using *our* is even that high. This is not just a matter of semantics, but an illustration of the broader phenomenon that youth don't feel connected to the people and the system governing their lives, that they don't feel a sense of ownership or agency.

The irony is that when asked about issues young people actually want *more* from government, not less—even if they do not employ that precise phrase. Hart's survey found a large majority in favor of hiring more teachers and reducing class sizes and strengthening and preserving Social Security, government assistance for low-income families, and even prescription drug coverage for senior citizens. Only 23 percent said that smaller government should be a top or high priority for the nation. This survey was conducted before the events of September 11, which, temporarily at least, swelled the admiration for and trust in government among young people.

The ambivalence about politics is also reflected in career choices. Half of all those surveyed thought it was very important to choose a profession that contributes to society, but only one-quarter were very or even fairly interested in government service. I'm sure that reflects the growing attraction of careers in the nonprofit world, seen as more noble and interesting than the labyrinthine corridors of the federal bureaucracy. It's not necessarily that young people are more cynical about government, or more alienated, as other research has shown. It's that they don't see politics and government as relevant to their lives.

Again, test this hypothesis. Ask a teenager what government does. See if he or she recognizes that it picks up the trash every week, clears the snow, provides running water and sewage lines, maintains the local ball field and swimming pool, fixes the high school roof and the giant springtime craters in the road, pays for the cops and crossing guards. Government isn't only grand pronouncements from Washington about homeland security and Medicare. Government is the silent glue that knits together our communities and helps maintain our extraordinary standard of living—not always as efficiently and honestly as it should, but with a day-in, day-out consistency that most of us take for granted, especially if you don't earn enough to pay taxes. Occasionally, it even solves problems, but most young people don't believe that, either.

* * *

So we've birthed a generation that knows little about the way government works and therefore thinks it is irrelevant, a generation that's heard decades of anti-government rhetoric and therefore thinks it's the cause of problems and not a solution, a generation that rationally directs its civic energies elsewhere and considers voting a lifestyle option, not a civic responsibility.

This is not a happy situation, but it has not gone unnoticed in the world of education. Political scientists bemoan the illiteracy of this generation, while civic activists argue that more should happen in the classroom. A growing cadre of people devoted to service learning are realizing that the *service* is too often divorced from the *learning,* while every day, it seems, a new do-good organization has posted a website designed to get young people involved. Politicians, scholars, judges, even the president are saying that the nation's schools must reclaim their mission to produce graduates who are citizens, and to take civic education to a more significant and innovative level. As "The Civic Mission of Schools" (CMS) report noted, "There has been common interest in increasing youth civic engagement but no common ground as to how to do this effectively."

Now that common ground is being tilled. Thanks in large

measure to the powerful punch packed into the forty-page CMS report, ratified as it was by a broad range of stakeholders, those who care about this issue have a blueprint on how to proceed. No longer can we say that we like the house in theory, but don't know how to build it. The directions for construction are starting to emerge.

"The truth is, we know that civic education in schools works," says Peter Levine, CIRCLE's deputy director. "We know that when we teach kids, they actually learn, and they get better at it."

The report suggests first that there be agreement on the goals. Civic education should help students become competent, responsible citizens who are informed and thoughtful, participate in their communities, act politically, and have moral and civic virtues. Note the choice of words here. "Acting politically" isn't necessarily running for office. It's organizing your neighbors to protest a new liquor store coming to the avenue, or participating in a school committee dealing with drug abuse. This is "political" like apple pie is dessert, as wholesome as it comes. The promotion of virtues isn't only something the preacher talks about on Sunday; moral and civic virtue helps us strike a balance between our personal interests and beliefs and the common good. Moreover, the goal here is for students to acquire not only content but to acquire skills. It's not enough to know they should vote, or even know how to vote—that hardly sets us apart from authoritarian regimes where turnout is a dependable 99.9 percent and the outcome is never in doubt. What's essential are those other qualities so classically American, the *chutzpah* of citizens willing to challenge authority, take charge, take a risk.

Schools are not the only purveyors of this wisdom, and the report duly notes that families and religious institutions play a proven role in promoting youth civic participation. Vote, and your children are more likely to; attend religious services regularly, and your children will volunteer more, feel they can "make a difference," and view government in a more positive light. But those institutions, too, have been loosening their hold on youth and, to some degree, shirking their responsibilities. Can we depend on families to nurture new citizens when half of the adults in America don't vote? Political parties are surely not going to offer their services, for all the reasons we've explored earlier. Popular culture celebrates materialism, selfishness, violence, and belly-button piercing. Need I say more?

Schools are the place for civic education, and not only by default. They are the constant institution in a child's life, and are able to create within their community a testing ground for the real civic challenges and opportunities that await each graduate. As the CMS report noted, in the past many scholars doubted that civic education classes and programs were effective. Now, an impressive body of statistical evidence drawn from national surveys and testing assessments indicates that classroom discussions of issues, courses on history and government that engage students in active learning, and other forms of civic education can improve students' civic knowledge, skills, and intentions to vote and volunteer. As Peter Levine says, we know it can work.

Unfortunately, this necessary, efficacious feature of education is being squeezed out of curriculums and zeroed out of school budgets. Between 1988 and 1998, the proportion of fourth graders who reported taking social studies daily fell from 49 percent to 39 percent. By the time those students reach high school, the only offering is usually a "government" class, which describes and analyzes government in an official, rather than participatory way; the traditional civics class emphasizing rights and responsibilities has all but disappeared. The reasons are sadly obvious: the obsession with testing for verbal and mathematical skills has overpowered other educational initiatives; school-based extracurricular programs are often the first target of budget cuts; and teachers fear criticism—even litigation—if their classroom policy conversations stray into partisan trouble.

In contrast to previous generations, young people today also have fewer opportunities to practice politics in student government. According to research conducted by Kent Jennings and Laura Stoker, half of those who were eighteen years old in 1965 ran for an elected office in high school, but only 27 percent of their children did in 1997. Sixty-three percent of the baby boomers served as an officer in some sort of school organization; only 44 percent of their children did. And 88 percent of the older crowd were members of an organization outside of school, while only 41 percent of their children were.

Although these trends are widespread, they are not uniform, and the disparities among schools are also cause for concern. The CMS report noted that the level of civic knowledge, skills, and attitudes differ among students of different demographic backgrounds. That finding is based on rigorous national surveys, and I can offer only a powerful anecdote that confirms it. I asked my class at Penn to read the CMS report and then reflect on their own high school experiences, in and outside the classroom. The conversation surprised us all. This relatively homogeneous collection of Ivy League undergrads had widely varied experiences, ranging from the ridiculous to the sublime. In some high schools, students were able to take advantage of numerous civics-related classes and extracurricular activities, including student court, mock United Nations, literary magazines, and student councils that tackled charged and important issues. Blake Stuchin went to a private school in Manhattan that boasted thirty-one different student-run publications and so prized these activities that the last hour of each school day was allotted for club meetings. And this was before sports practice began.

In other high schools, student political empowerment was limited to selecting a venue for the prom, elections were often treated as a joke, and the chance to participate in national civic programs were rarely offered. "Students got turned off to government because student government didn't do anything," reported Paul Townsend, who went to school in suburban Philadelphia.

Listening to this freewheeling conversation, a trend immediately became apparent: The civic experience of a student was often directly related to the wealth and resources of his or her high school. Simply put, private high schools and well-endowed public ones offered an impressive array of opportunities, while less advantaged schools with limited resources offered little or nothing at all. Two students at two different schools who participated in sports were actually barred from joining any student government clubs. You could be either a jock or a government nerd, but not both.

Ben Cruse experienced the difference between schools firsthand. He began ninth grade in a large public high school in Hartford, Connecticut, that was crumbling, literally, inside and out. Four-fifths of his freshmen class was expected to drop out by senior year. No one brought books to class. Teachers were overwhelmed. "Student government didn't do anything," he recalled. "In a place like that, you don't really want to hang around for after-school activities."

When the school lost its accreditation in the middle of the year, Cruse's parents decided to send him to Kingswood-Oxford, a prep school only a mile and a half away. Not only was the physical environment a stunning departure from what he had known—with well-manicured lawns, large trees, student lounges—the civic atmosphere was, too. Outside the classroom was an active student government and model United Nations; in the classroom, politics was constantly discussed and voter registration encouraged. Cruse's advanced placement political science course was taught by a college professor. The contrast between the two schools amazes him to this day.

Empirically we know that resources don't determine everything, for there are marvelous civic programs happening in some of the poorest urban schools, as I'll describe shortly. But in many schools, resources help foster a sense of entitlement, the expectation that a culture of empowerment is a natural state of affairs. It's a marvelous expectation to have, as long as it is equitably available.

There are other reasons for this hodgepodge of experiences. State policies have a huge influence on civic education because there is so little national standardization, and a report released by the National Center for Learning and Citizenship in November 2003 revealed that wide variation exists from state to state. While thirty-nine states require a course in government or civics for high school graduation, for instance, only five of those states require students to pass an exit exam that includes social studies to graduate. (The five are Georgia, Louisiana, Mississippi, New Mexico, and New York; several other states are set to institute such a requirement.)

Interestingly, this is an option favored by students themselves. When research done by CIRCLE in 2002 asked young people whether civics and government classes should be required in high school, the answer was a resounding yes. Naturally, support was weakest among the younger respondents, those ages fifteen to seventeen who would presumably have to take such classes, but nearly 70 percent of their slightly older peers thought this was a fine idea. The racial group most in favor, by the way, was African-American women.

* * *

But what kind of civic education do we need? The CMS report is quite clear that we should not return to the past, to the lectures on the arcane details of federal legislative procedures that bypass the chance to wrestle with larger public issues and underlying principles. Knowledge is important, both morally and practically; we know, for instance, that the more knowledgeable adults are the more likely they will vote on issues rather than just personalities. Effective civic education should include instruction in government, history, law, and democracy, but it must incorporate discussion of issues and events that are relevant to the students' lives. "Much depends on the quality of the discussion," the report warns. "Just as we oppose rote instruction on the minutiae of legislative procedure, so we object to unstructured, uninformed, or uncivil discussions of current issues. Conversations should be carefully moderated so that students feel welcome to speak from a variety of perspectives, with mutual respect and civility."

Service learning—as opposed to service only—should also be part of the package. The difference between the two is the connection to the curriculum. Service learning enables the volunteer work to be put into sociological and political context, to understand that there are solutions to problems that go beyond what one goodhearted person can do. Like so much else in the educational arena, service learning is still a work in progress, but in general research suggests that students who participate in quality programs exhibit improved civic skills and attitudes and may even be more likely to vote as adults. Service as a subject is also much more complicated to organize and teach, which is why so many stressed schools have resorted to mandating volunteer hours rather than taking this next, necessary step.

One of the most important recommendations made in the

CMS report is to view civic education as something that occurs outside the classroom as effectively as inside. This may seem obvious to the prep school with the thirty-one publications, but all too many of the nation's schools have paid precious little attention to activities that promote the skills of citizenship and sometimes, due to budget cuts, have canceled student government and newspapers altogether. (Athletic skills are rarely overlooked; sports is one of the few extracurricular activities that have become more common since 1965, but research has found that student athletes tend to be *less* likely to vote and become politically engaged.) Giving students the chance to run their own council, have a say in the management of the school, express themselves through a school newspaper, and organize according to issues and concerns is as vital as teaching them the details of the Constitution. These activities create a school culture of debate and exploration, with the added benefit of nurturing self-esteem and developing identity just when students need to the most.

This kind of civic education has inherent risks, especially in schools where a command-and-control structure is needed to maintain safety and discipline. "We have to become more tolerant of things that go wrong when you have a culture of debate," says Peter Levine. A strong school leadership must be brave enough to take those risks, and a strong community wise enough to lend its support. The writers of this report weren't just dreaming, however. Examples of such innovation are found around the nation.

* * *

There's a sweet story on the website of Kids Voting USA that tells how three businessmen from Arizona traveled to Costa Rica on a fishing trip in 1988 and discovered that the American electorate did not measure up at all to this small Central American country. About 80 percent of Costa Ricans turn out to vote, which they attribute to the tradition of children accompanying their parents to the polls. "Youths learn early the importance of voting in a democracy," the website says. "As a result, Costa Ricans believe their form of government is well preserved for the future."

This idea might be news to the Costa Ricans, but that's not quite the point here. The enthralled businessmen brought the idea back home to Arizona and parlayed it into a national civic education curriculum that, thankfully, goes beyond what they observed of Costa Rican democracy while they were catching fish. The act of taking one's child to vote is a splendid one (especially in November, when they can be plied with leftover Halloween candy), but it is not, by itself, a ticket to active citizenship. A ten-year-old might go willingly, a sixteen-year-old only accompanies his parents anywhere under extreme duress, and a twenty-year-old is unlikely to go to the polls on the strength of a childhood memory.

Kids Voting USA has become a nationally recognized model for promoting citizenship because it starts early, engages families, ties into a solid curriculum, and recognizes that as much as anything, voting is a social behavior best reinforced at home. "The real power happens around the interplay between children and parents," says Christopher E. Heller, president and CEO.

The program, which organizers say now reaches 4.3 million students nationwide, is designed as a community effort, requiring the input of local business leaders, journalists, educators, and election officials. A community Kids Voting affiliate raises funds, prints ballots, and recruits poll volunteers to greet and assist students. The majority of Kids Voting students visit official polls on Election Day to participate in a process that replicates the adult process, although some are now using mail ballots and alternative forms of voting.

The action is not just on Election Day. Students as young as first graders are exposed to the concepts of democracy in ways they can understand with, say, the Oreo lesson. The teacher will gather children in the center of the room as if they were getting ready to go off to the polls, then ask a few students to step into the corner because they aren't eligible to vote. A few more will be sent to a different corner, since they aren't registered. The group is thinned further because some of them didn't bother to show up on Election Day. The teacher then tells the remaining children that they have to decide for the rest of the class whether they're going to have Oreos for a snack, or something else.

"And the six-, seven-, and eight-year-olds get it," says Heller. "They get the fact that they've forfeited the right to decide for themselves, and that the other students will decide what they're going to eat. I honestly believe that young people don't think that voting makes a difference. There aren't enough examples where it does matter."

Of course, the Oreo lesson is too simplistic for high school. Kids Voting is now developing a curriculum for older students called Destination Democracy, to provide a richer, ongoing experience for teenagers that isn't tied solely to elections. Here again, the focus is on making a link between learning in school and discussion at home. Michael McDevitt, a professor at the University of Colorado who has evaluated Kids Voting, calls it the "trickle-up influence." He contends that voting should be viewed more as a social activity than a civic one, a chance for students to become competent in an area of adult concern, thereby developing their own identity and self-esteem. So when a student is asked to interview his parents about their voting history, watch candidates debate together and discuss the is- sues, he is establishing his own political identity in the context of the family.

"Mathematically, you're not going to make a difference when you vote. I know I'm not supposed to say that, but it's true," says McDevitt. "I look at citizenship as a mechanism of personal expression, to get young people to understand that they vote because it's an expression of their values. There's an implication that young people are permanently disengaged and are purposely opting out of the political system. I don't think so. Instead, there's no social motivation for them to care about politics. What I've found with Kids Voting is that the family as a social unit can be very effective."

How effective? McDevitt's evaluation in 2001 found that increased attention to campaign news represented *the* strongest effect of the intervention, cutting across demographic categories. "All types of students develop curiosity in the classroom that translates into increased attention to campaign events, candidates, and issues. This mental effort endures as a long-term consequence of Kids Voting," he concluded. Another study he published in 2003 found that "school-family bonding" was markedly enhanced by Kids Voting, creating "a loop of influence in which the family and school enliven the political discussion of each other." In one particular site, El Paso County, Colorado, the gap in civic involvement between white and Latino students was narrowed. Earlier studies of Kids Voting also found a change in parental behavior: They were more apt to discuss the election with friends, have strong opinions, and support politics. Voting precincts that had implemented the program for one election cycle demonstrated a voter turnout 5 percent higher than comparison precincts, and turnout was boosted by another 2 percent after a second election cycle.

The International Institute for Democracy and Electoral Assistance (IDEA) report on the global decline of youth political participation selected Kids Voting as one of four case studies highlighting what can be done to reverse the trend. The evaluators were impressed by the program's community leadership component, range of actors, strong media support, and its connection to school curricula.

True, these aren't blockbuster results, just the slow, steady improvements one can hope to make in turning around decades of neglect and detachment. Kids Voting costs, but not much; it averages fifty cents to a dollar per child. That's a rather modest investment for a program that knows how to make hope in the political process habit-forming.

* * *

Phyllis Kaniss has long gone against the grain in her academic research, writing about local media when everyone else studied the national press corps, so it was natural that she'd do the same when conceiving a project on youth civic engagement. "So many important things happen locally," says Kaniss, a member of the Annenberg School of Communications at the University of Pennsylvania and national director of Student Voices. "We wanted the students to look at their neighborhoods and see what's around them, and then bring them to the election through the things they care about. I'm absolutely convinced that you have to start close to home."

Home is Philadelphia, where there's no shortage of cynicism about the political process, and for good reason. This is, after all, where the mayor was in a tight reelection campaign in 2003 against a worthy opponent—until the discovery of an FBI corruption probe in City Hall weeks before the election *boosted* his popularity and propelled him to a landslide victory. You can understand why young people think their local government is either a joke or an embarrassment and hardly an inspiration.

Inspiration, though, is what this well-regarded civics program is intended to create—that, and knowledgeable students confident enough to question candidates directly, engage one another on significant issues, speak publicly, and become active citizens in their community. Beginning with the 1999 Philadelphia mayoral race, and then expanding nationally, Student Voices employs modern Internet technology, engaged teachers, and old-fashioned, shoe-leather research to insert students into the political discussion and help them become critical thinkers about the challenges facing urban America.

Here's what was happening during one, albeit unusually busy day in the midst of Philadelphia's primary election season for mayor and City Council. On May 6, 2003, at 7:30 in the morning, Student Voices co-sponsored with the League of Women Voters, the school district, and other groups a voter registration assembly at George Washington High School in the city's Northeast section. As eligible seniors were encouraged to register to vote, Student Voices students made their own presentation about the importance of voting. At 9:30 that morning, Republican mayoral candidate Sam Katz visited an SV class at Edison High School in North Philly to talk with students about the city's challenges. Then in the evening, starting at six o'clock, Student Voices co-sponsored a forum in Center City for at-large city council candidates, which was co-moderated by a young participant in the program. Meeting the candidates face-to-face is an empowering experience for any citizen, and for the young it noticeably makes them more impressed and less cynical about those who are running for public office. Plus, it highlights the wisdom of focusing locally—it's far easier to persuade a city council candidate to visit a high school classroom than someone running for president of the United States.

In the backdrop to all these public activities is a constant, on-line dialogue about urban issues driven by the students' concerns and tailored to their communities. On a given day, the Philadelphia website hosted a discussion about a proposed law to regulate campaign contributions and a debate on how to attract supermarkets to blighted neighborhoods. Students in Newark, New Jersey, were asked how they would improve the city's high schools. In Tulsa, the subject was gangs; in Denver, school vouchers.

And in Seattle, a Student Voices class at Middle College Northgate High School, an alternative school for at-risk kids, became part of a serious political debate over the revitalization of the fifty-eight-year-old mall that is home to the school and what has been described as a "sea of asphalt." The class researched the contentious mall development plans and decided to push Seattle's mayor and city council to create a citizen's advisory commission for the project. While they were at it, the students requested that one of them be a member of the commission; after all, they were mall "stakeholders" as much as nearby homeowners and businessmen.

The Student Voices teacher, Karen Hansen, found out that the city council was planning to act on the Northgate plan only hours before the scheduled meeting on December 8, 2003, and she was able to bring only one student with her, the youngest and shyest girl in her class. Perhaps it was fitting that the quietest child was suddenly in the limelight—not only did the council and mayor agree to put a student on the new advisory commission, but the council president publicly praised student and teacher by name at the meeting.

"I guess it was one of my proudest moments as a teacher that because of my kids' initiative, they had now become policy makers at the highest level in the city. It just blew me away!" Hansen wrote in an e-mail the next morning. "When I told the rest of the class today, they were busting their buttons. They now have proof that 'student voices' are indeed heard in this city."

These are children who never thought anyone in power listened to them, and now they have reason to believe otherwise. Evaluation of Student Voices has shown that its participants subsequently increased their registration and voting, but it's obviously too small and limited a program to make sweeping predictions. This is labor-intensive civic education, dependent on teachers willing to be engaged enough to go to city council meetings on a cold December evening. Kaniss has received funding to take the program, now only in a handful of cities, across Pennsylvania for the 2004–2005 school year, a mammoth leap. The expansion will be telling. Even so, it's evident that a carefully constructed program can inspire students in some of the nation's most disadvantaged schools to become full participants in their civic and political communities. We know this can work.

*   *   *

David Hall is one of the exceptions of his generation: a twenty-nine-year-old who has never missed voting in an election, who has already made a run for public office, and who still is amazed that he saw Nelson Mandela speak ten years ago, before the great man was elected president of South Africa. Hall did a lot of volunteering as a teenager, and then experienced what he called "an awakening," the realization that there had to be a public policy component to address the social issues he thought he was helping to ameliorate. Sparking that same sense of discovery drives him now as a teacher.

"Inspiring young people to vote is a passion of mine," says Hall, who teaches twelfth-grade civics at North Penn High School, a sprawling, demographically mixed high school in Lansdale, Pennsylvania. "I believe the most important reason that we have schools is to create good citizens. If we don't teach children about their rights, then they don't have them. If we don't teach them what happened in history, then it never happened—at least as far as they are concerned."

When it comes to answering the big question—that is, what kind of civics education do we need?—Hall is just as adamant. Loading up the lesson with dry content has serious limitations, because it exaggerates the *how much* at the expense of the *how*.

It's far more important and efficacious to engage students in what he terms "a conversation with democracy" and get them to discover on their own the beauty (and the challenges) of our distinctive form of self-governance. "I feel strongly that you don't teach democracy, you experience it," he says.

His classroom model is called We the People: Project Citizen, designed by the Center for Civic Education (CCE), yet another national organization doing fine work in this field. Hall's class generally chooses its own topic to research—child abuse, college tuition costs, gun violence, you name it—then it must understand the issues, devise a solution, and create an action plan to change whatever part of the law needs changing. The last part of the assignment is key, because it forces the students to go further than most citizens do in not only proposing solutions but exploring how they can be implemented, how change can really be made. The class then presents its findings to a panel of local judges, including some elected officials, if Hall can persuade them to attend. This accomplishes what other successful civic education programs do: It forces people in power to listen to the voices of students. Hall usually requests that he *not* be given North Penn's honor students so that he can teach the kids who aren't born to the privilege of empowerment and haven't been raised to believe that they can make a difference in their communities.

At the end of the project in 2002 he surveyed his ninety-eight students and was so proud of the results that he sent me an e-mail chart with the findings. Before the class, 31 percent believed that they could *not* change public policy, 19 percent believed they could, and 49 percent were undecided. Afterward, only 10 percent felt their efforts would go to waste, and a full 66 percent believed that they could actually have an effect on government policy. (The rest were undecided.)

David Hall's enthusiasm for this approach is shared; 97 percent of the teachers surveyed in an evaluation of Project Citizen said they thought it was a good way to teach civic education—a finding that CCE proudly displays on its website, so like all such evaluations, it must be taken with a few grains of salt. And just because many of Hall's students have come to believe they can influence public policy doesn't guarantee that, when the time comes, they will exercise the franchise responsibly, although he is convinced that his students eventually vote in higher numbers than their peers.

Still, it is a bold and admirable start. Project Citizen is also being utilized in Bosnia and Herzegovina, in Latvia and Lithuania—places where democracy's roots are younger and more tenuous. Yet even though Hall has the solid backing of his department chair and principal, he is the only teacher at North Penn High orchestrating a civic experience like Project Citizen—it takes a certain mind-set, a willingness to court controversy and share classroom power. This kind of active learning requires teachers to trust their students—to pick a topic, manage their time, create a final project worthy of display before esteemed outsiders—and to risk the chance that the classroom conversation will veer off into potentially dangerous territory. "Many teachers fear controversy," Hall says. "My experience is that dealing with controversy is one of the reasons we have schools. I can't imagine my classroom without it."

Dealing with controversy is also one of the main reasons we have a democracy, but conflict and differences are too often ignored, repressed, or shunned by teachers, students *and* parents. As "The Civic Mission of Schools" report notes, "One of the most commonly identified barriers to teaching civic content and skills effectively is the fear of censure or controversy that many schools and teachers face if these issues are discussed with students."

It's time we broke down these barriers, and teach our children enough about the democracy they are inheriting to give them a reason to vote.

CHAPTER SEVEN

Virgin Voters:
What will it take to get
young people engaged?

Wednesday at noon on a warm Washington day, and a dozen or so people were sitting around a large conference table in a downtown office building. The regular monthly meeting of the Youth Vote Coalition was about to begin as more people arrived, taking every available chair around the table and lining the adjacent walls. Soon it felt like a cross between a corporate board meeting, a college seminar, and a pep rally. It was hard not to be impressed.

One by one the participants went around the room, introducing themselves by name and organization, sharing news about a university symposium on civic engagement and a reenactment of the Freedom Rides. They were so earnest and public-spirited, you'd think that the ghosts of Benjamin Franklin and James Dewey and Susan B. Anthony were hovering about, feeding them lines, urging them not to waver.

But I'm not sure the Founding Fathers and Mothers would have expected to see a representative from World Wrestling Entertainment address so august a group, and be received so warmly. Especially since he was there to announce the launch of "Smackdown Your Vote!," a new collaboration between professional wrestlers and hip-hop artists pledging to draw "Two Million More in 2004." Is this for real?

Dewey and Anthony likely would have been horrified to hear Teresa Van Deusen of Austin, Texas, unveil the latest marketing tool to get young people to the polls. (Franklin, I bet, would have chuckled). "This is bubblegum America," Van Deusen assured us as she rolled out the banner, pens, and trinkets brightly decorated with sixties' mod-style flowers and her new slogan:

Voter Virgin. Everybody's Doin' It in '04.

Welcome to the new world of promoting civic engagement. It involves wrestlers, hip-hop artists, sexy marketing, and every other tool imaginable to reach the nation's most technologically sophisticated and publicity-saturated generation. Playing "Yankee Doodle" isn't going to work anymore. Play Madonna, you might have a chance.

Or so the theory goes. The list of organizations attempting to connect young people with the political process grows longer every month, ranging from well-researched initiatives funded by major foundations to mainstays like Rock the Vote, to whimsical ideas like Voter Virgin. It's a comforting sign that the entrepreneurial spirit is alive and well, thanks largely to the Internet's ability to organize interest groups and disseminate information and market ideas, so that a student in Topeka can purchase a voter toolkit on-line from Texas and use it to push the election of a guy from Massachusetts. Whether these energetic but disparate efforts are effective is another matter. Given the poor state of this generation's civic health, and the urgency of the cause, it's time for a more rigorous search for what actually works and a commitment then to implement it.

Trouble is, everyone involved in civic renewal is awfully nice and well intentioned, and no one you'd want to criticize. Nor is anyone abusing their power or scheming to amass great resources by trying to persuade young people to vote (although a few entities undoubtedly see great marketing potential in attaching their names to such efforts). The decline in political engagement will not be stemmed by a single program or approach; if there were a "magic cure," it would already have been found and bottled by a savvy activist or political candidate. The promises of those pushing a simple solution—if students could only recite the Pledge of Allegiance every day, if they only were able to vote on-line—must be greeted with the same skepticism we show toward diet claims accompanied by preposterous before-and-after photographs. America's civic life will not suddenly get in shape with a $29.99 monthly plan.

This is about altering human behavior and the cultural norms that influence it, but before that seems too grand a task, remember that the landscape has changed in only thirty years' time, and redirecting these trends is entirely within our control. In my lifetime, less than half a century, cigarette smoking has gone from an acceptable, even ubiquitous thing-you-did to something shunned in most public places. Recycling certain products has become intuitive. Awareness of the hazards of getting behind the wheel of an automobile while intoxicated has not eradicated the scourge of drunk driving, but it has sharply curtailed it and reaped shame (and long prison sentences) on violators.

This is possible, as long as we *really* listen to what young people are saying, respect their motivations, and join with them to reform a system that, in the end, will work better for all of us.

The guiding principles: Clear away the obstacles. Make it personal. And above all, give them a reason to vote.

* * *

For a snapshot of the confused landscape for youth voting in the United States today, check out a report released in July 2003 by the National Association of Secretaries and States and the Youth Vote Coalition. With precise language and understandable graphics, the report gives a state-by-state accounting of a few basic procedures that we know would encourage youth political participation: same-day registration, allowing young people to work the polls on Election Day, youth outreach programs. The picture is slightly different in every state.

That's how it is meant to be in a federalist system, but the reliance on state decision making on matters of the franchise has long been an effective cover for resisting reform. Truth is, if the American establishment genuinely wanted to eliminate the barriers that have kept eligible citizens, especially young ones, from the polls, it could do so with a national movement that would build upon the best practices of the states. Far from being a novel approach, this is exactly what happened when every other modernization of the suffrage movement occurred. Individual states had long given women and blacks and eighteen-year-olds the right to vote before the franchise was extended nationwide. We should follow that pattern today to ensure that our electoral process is accessible to all, especially to a younger population prone to move around the corner and across the country.

Only 13 percent of the states have laws allowing eligible voters to register on Election Day. What is stopping the other 87 percent from adopting a change that is proven to increase turnout without the nasty side effects of fraud that some people fear? As Thomas Patterson notes in *The Vanishing Voter,* Minnesota went to same-day registration in the 1970s and since then has led the nation in voter turnout. This isn't just a reward to procrastinators; allowing citizens to register on Election Day makes it more likely they will remember to both register *and* vote. And contrary to certain conventional political wisdom, it does not swell the rolls of low-income Democrats (a reason Republicans have long resisted such a reform). That same argument was initially used to block the Motor Voter Act of 1993, but the prediction was incorrect, for in fact the new voters were evenly divided between both parties.

So unless you live in Minnesota or Idaho, Maine, New Hampshire, Wisconsin, or Wyoming—in other words, the states smart enough to allow same-day registration—I would suggest that you lobby with all your might for this simple, powerful reform. (North Dakota has no registration requirement at all, a progressive step that is just about impossible to imagine in a state with more people.)

Residents of seven other states have an added target—the state laws that require a first-time voter to cast a ballot in person. In Illinois, Michigan, Louisiana, Nevada, Tennessee, Virginia, and West Virginia, this effectively disenfranchises college students away from home on their first election, since they are prohibited from filing an absentee ballot. The modern-day rationale for this eludes me.

Another obstacle that should be easily swept away: restrictive voting hours. As Patterson notes, the Sturm und Drang on election night 2000 over the network's irresponsible behavior in Florida obscured a more important fact: The polls in the Sunshine State close at 7 P.M. In fact, Florida is one of twenty-six states that require citizens to vote by 7:30 P.M. local time *or earlier*. (The other states are Alabama, Arizona, Arkansas, Colorado, Georgia, Hawaii, Illinois, Indiana, Kansas, Kentucky, Mississippi, Missouri, Nevada, New Hampshire, New Mexico, North Carolina, Ohio, Oklahoma, South Carolina, Tennessee, Texas, Vermont, Virginia, West Virginia, and Wyoming).

Why, in a world that operates 24 hours, 7 days a week, do we permit polling places to close earlier than some neighborhood banks?

Limits on polling hours are a time-tested way of discouraging working people from casting a ballot, and it's also a fine strategy to deter young people, who very likely are at a job, in class all day, or only waking up when the rest of us are ready to retire. No coincidence, then, that in the 2000 presidential election turnout in states with early closing times was three percentage points lower on average than in states where the polls didn't close until 8 P.M. or later, according to Patterson.

Second on the to-do list: Challenge your states' polling hours to make this central act of citizenship more available to more people.

Next, if we were truly serious about removing obstacles to the franchise, we'd follow the recommendation of a bipartisan national commission and turn Election Day into a national holiday, which would have the added benefit of increasing the availability of poll workers and polling places. This bipartisan commission wasn't just any group, but the nineteen-member National Commission on Federal Election Reform created after the 2000 election debacle and chaired by former presidents Gerald Ford and Jimmy Carter. Lest you complain that establishing another national holiday in November is ludicrous, understand that the commission suggested merging Election Day with Veterans Day, a neat way of honoring those who served the nation by tying their sacrifice with every citizen's obligation. And lest anyone think about criticizing the commission for dismissing veterans, remember that Ford and Carter served in the active military.

Unfortunately, this smart, simple solution was beaten back by interest groups holding on to a fading memory of Veterans Day rather than accepting what it has become, which is largely an excuse for a three-day weekend and department store sales. Congress never even had the chance to debate the suggestion, but that doesn't mean it should go the way of the GI Bill, into the pile of fine examples of American problem solving consigned to history's dustbin.

* * *

Even though these reforms in voting practices require state and national legislative action, they may be the simplest to accomplish. As Chris Heller of Kids Voting USA says, "The mechanics are the easy part. It's the motivation that's missing."

How to motivate this generation to vote, given that politicians ignore them, community service is more rewarding, and government feels irrelevant? It may be that the most effective way is simply to ask them.

Like a ship sailing farther and farther out to sea, politics has lost its relationship to the land of its birth (and its berth) during the last thirty years. It used to be a process you could touch, and in some places it still is—if you are lucky enough to live in New Hampshire or Iowa during a contested presidential primary, or in city like Philadelphia when Ed Rendell, that most tactile of politicians, was mayor. Once, political parties provided the connection that could be seen and heard and experienced; now, politics is largely a spectator sport, conducted on television and before niche audiences chosen with the precision of smart-bomb technology.

The need to get personal is most compelling for young voters. That this is nothing new makes the insight all the more heartbreaking. Consider this snippet from a story in a well-known newsweekly:

> *To attract the attention of unregistered persons, both parties use posters, bumper stickers, manuals, letters, tapes sent to radio stations, advertisements in student newspapers.*
>
> *However, party officials say that these methods bring questionable results. It is face-to-face contact between party worker and prospective registrant—plus follow-up phone calls and even transportation to an election office—that gets effective results.*
>
> *According to Mary Lou Burg, former vice chairman of the Democratic National Committee, nothing succeeds like door-to-door canvassing.*

The source? *U.S. News & World Report,* August 28, 1972.

I'll let the political scientists and historians debate how Americans lost sight of this basic wisdom, but at least some activists are not afraid to go back to the future, and a few researchers are arming them with proof that door-to-door can-vassing works even in a network age.

The best, most conclusive study is one done by Donald P. Green, Alan S. Gerber, and David W. Nickerson, all of Yale University. Unlike much of the research done about young people and voting, theirs was conducted according to the gold standard, as a randomized experiment in which those treated with the "intervention" were compared to a control group in several different settings. This study was conducted before the November 6, 2001, elections in Bridgeport, Columbus, Detroit, Minneapolis, St. Paul, and Raleigh. Registered voters of all ages were randomly assigned to two groups. Those in the first group received a personal visit from someone representing a coalition of nonpartisan student and community organizations, encouraging them to vote. The second group got no visits. After the election, voting records (a much more accurate indicator than self-reporting) were used to compare the turnout rates in both groups and also to see whether the intervention affected anyone living at the same address as those contacted personally. The study then looked more closely at voters under age twenty-five.

All of this was taking place in cities that had varied experiences on that Election Day. In Bridgeport, races for the school board and city council didn't generate much voter interest, while in Detroit a closely contested mayoral race drew a lot of attention. In St. Paul, the mayoral campaign was so competitive that only 400 votes eventually distinguished the winner from the loser. The Raleigh case study turned out to be the most problematic; informational materials arrived late and the mostly African-American canvassers were not warmly welcomed by some white residents. The results from that city did not match the others.

Nonetheless, Green, Gerber, and Nickerson had a powerful story to tell when the votes were tabulated and analyzed. "Each successful contact with a young registrant raises the probability of turnout by roughly 8–12 percentage points. This figure, it should be noted, is a conservative estimate," they wrote. What they called "the spillover effect" was even greater, especially if the person contacted had young housemates. This was especially impressive given the meager budgets on which these campaigns operated, they noted, proving that this sort of personal attention does not require vast amounts of resources. If campaign workers were hired at $10 an hour and made eight contacts an hour, the cost-per-vote would be $15.

That's cheap compared to direct mail, phone banks, and costly television ads. "Those seeking to do something about low voter turnout rates have a proven, if old-fashioned, method for increasing turnout," they concluded.

A smaller study conducted in Fresno, California, in the weeks before the 2002 election emphasized this point with the nation's most ignored slice of the electorate, young Latino voters. Melissa R. Michelson of California State University found that face-to-face canvassing improved turnout, especially if the canvasser was also Latino.

Based on the strength of these studies, the Pew Charitable Trusts is throwing more than $4 million and its reputation behind what it considers the largest grassroots effort to mobilize eighteen- to twenty-four-year-olds. The nonpartisan New Voters Project hopes to register 260,000 young people in 2004 and to increase their average turnout in the November presidential election by 5 percent, or about 100,000 new voters. They plan to do this the old-fashioned way. Organized by George Washington University's Graduate School of Political Management and working through Public Interest Research Groups (PIRGs) and networks of activists, about three hundred workers in six states will personally register new voters, build files and accumulate contact information, canvass door-to-door, and on Election Day get them to the polls.

"We have been studying youth voting interventions since 1999, and found that the best approach is the peer-to-peer ask," says Tobi Walker, the Pew program officer for the project. "This is Grassroots Organizing 101. We know what it takes to get them to vote, the power of the personal ask."

This nuts-and-bolts approach borrows from a traditional political campaign's "Get Out the Vote" techniques and targets them to young voters, an audience that, as we know, politicians rarely try to reach. Ivan Frishberg, spokesman for the project, believes that the old excuses for ignoring young voters—they move around, they're hard to contact, they're unpredictable—will be proven wrong. Although the project is nonpartisan, it will share its voter information files with any political parties, interest groups, or causes willing to follow through with a message. It will be up to the campaigns to take the next step.

Frishberg was one of the founders of the Youth Vote Coalition in 1994 and swore he'd stay away from the subject this election cycle. That is, until the New Voters Project came along. "If you ask them, they will vote," he says, "and we're going to directly ask a million young people."

*   *   *

The New Voters Project is, essentially, a ground war in the battle for the youth vote and for that reason, it stands alone, tilling virgin territory. Up in the skies, on the airwaves, is a different story. There it's downright congested.

The air war began when Rock the Vote was launched in 1990 by members of the recording industry, who pioneered the use of rock stars, youth venues, and the Internet to register and mobilize young voters. Two years later, it partnered with MTV and its Choose or Lose campaign, which sends a street team around the country to interview young voters and the candidates who are supposed to represent them. By the 2000 presidential election, World Wrestling Entertainment parlayed its popular televised matches into Smackdown the Vote! Four years later, WWE and Russell Simmons's Hip-Hop Summit Action Network combined their powerful celebrity forces to launch a "2 Million More in '04 Campaign." Also in 2004, Norman Lear, the television producer who brought Archie Bunker into American living rooms, gathered up many of his Hollywood celebrity friends and launched Declare Yourself, another high-octane effort to get young people out to vote.

As Gary Davis, vice president of corporate communications for the WWE, told the Youth Vote Coalition meeting that day, "The best way to get them to the polls is to get them off the couch."

These are not inexpensive endeavors; Lear alone raised $27 million in private and corporate donations. In a society dominated by celebrity, for a generation powered by its pop culture, the sight of actress Drew Barrymore, rapper Rev Run, or wrestler Maven Huffman urging young people to vote may do for the electoral process what Michael Jordan did for sneaker sales. Or not. The effectiveness of these media efforts is difficult to measure, especially when they are targeting the same demographic at the same time. It's possible to track how many young people registered to vote through a specific website or event. Choose or Lose claims to have signed up two million new voters since it began; Smackdown the Vote boasts that it registered 150,000 voters for the 2000 presidential election and more than 400,000 since. At a Hip-Hop Summit in Philadelphia during the summer of 2003, 11,000 new voters were registered in just a few days. But there's no way of knowing whether those newly eligible voters actually cast a ballot, and if so, whether it was a massive, muscular wrestler or the latest smooth-tongued hip-hop star who inspired that vote on Election Day.

Would I have voted if the heroes of my youth told me to? If Paul Simon and Art Garfunkel had serenaded me about civic duty, or Carole King had persuaded me that I'd have a friend in the franchise?

Truth is, politics and celebrity have long had a symbiotic relationship, as movie stars and recording artists have used their magnetism and name recognition to entertain troops, rally voters and support causes, and used their talents to give voice to soulful political expression. It's hard to criticize today's celebrities from doing what others have done before them.

When announcing the partnership with the WWE, Russell Simmons, chairman of the Hip-Hop Summit Network, noted that many young people pay attention to the words of rappers Jay-Z, Eminem, 50 Cent, and Rev Run much more than they do any politician. Simmons's brother, the aforementioned Rev Run of the group Run-DMC, even broke into a rap on why young people should follow his lead on voting: "Preach on a Sunday, rap on a Monday. Y'all do what Run say, to get better one day." Added WWE star Maven Huffman, "A lot of young people look up to us. I can take that excitement and enthusiasm and turn it to voting."

Bless him for doing so. And bless Ben Stiller, Vince Vaughan, Cameron Diaz, Ed Norton, Michael Douglas, and the other megastars for joining in Lear's Declare Yourself mobilization effort. Lear is no stranger to civic activism, having started the advocacy group People for the American Way in 1981 and then taking his rare copy of the Declaration of Independence on a fifty-city tour beginning in 2000 to inspire Americans to vote. We can even applaud candidate Bill Clinton for appearing on MTV in 1992, a move that probably drove the slight uptick in youth voting during that presidential election campaign (although the presence of independent Ross Perot helped enormously, too).

Thanks to technology, today's younger generation is defined by popular culture as intensely as any generation that preceded it, and it only makes sense to use the culture's icons to mobilize new voters and create a buzz that politics is acceptable, if not essential. But the reach of even a mainstay like Rock the Vote is limited, and it's a mistake to rely too much on this strategy. "The notion of making political participation cool is great, but those groups don't have the budget to do the kind of saturation that Nike can, and Coca-Cola can," says Alison Byrne Fields, who worked with Rock the Vote from 1998 until 2001.

Those groups can effectively register new voters, both on-line and in person, at barber shops, rock concerts, and college fairs. They can sponsor debates and provide the kind of information a new voter needs to know where to go, what to do. Rock the Vote's pulsing website does everything from target young women ("Chicks Rock!") to sell baby-doll T-shirts emblazoned with its red, white, and blue logo for $14.99. On declareyourself.com, you can read about the history of the Declaration of Independence and watch the previews of a new video with Stiller and Vaughan. A gigantic, intricate web of information is being spun in cyberspace, linking many of these efforts and offering more information on voting and candidates than any one person can absorb.

Nonetheless, this is still politics from a distance, and it's still politics wrapped in commerce, the very attributes that have caused committed young people to forgo political engagement in favor of community service. National, nonpartisan mobilization efforts encourage young people *to* vote, but they don't provide a reason why, and when elections appear only every four years, these efforts do little to establish the habit of voting. Rock the Vote has tried in recent years to focus on off-year elections and has begun creating "street teams" to organize local grassroots campaigns and solicit new voters in person. RTV also has begun to target specific demographics, such as young

Latinos and gays and lesbians, often partnering with existing groups in certain regions.

But as one student leader in the organization told me, "It is typical for a grassroots campaign to grow into a national effort, but unusual for a national effort to, somewhat arbitrarily, turn to grassroots organizing. Involvement in local politics has been a by-product of the establishment of street teams, not the purpose." Rock the Vote's national name recognition is a tremendous asset, but it's unclear whether that can be grafted onto a sustained, meaningful local effort. And its attempts to appear "cool" may backfire. In 2000, RTV promoted a program telling young people to "Piss Off a Politician"—an edgy phrase, yes, but a potentially troubling message if the aim is to persuade the alienated and disengaged that politics and government are worth their while. As Kate Liberman, one of my students, noted, "There are plenty of ways to encourage people to get involved on an issue without demeaning the politicians elected to serve our country, or for that matter, demeaning active young citizens who do want to make a difference."

*   *   *

Another strategy is playing out in the world of civic good works, and it, too, is driven by only the best of intentions. Whether it can transform a generation, however, is an open question.

It speaks for what it calls "the September 11 Generation.... Too young to vote, old enough to lead." The group is called Freedom's Answer, a nonprofit, nonpartisan voter turnout campaign led by young people but organized by two old hands, Doug Bailey, a former Republican political strategist, and Mike McCurry, once President Clinton's press secretary. "How could we summon post 9-11 desire to do something for the common good into an idea that would make our democracy better?" they asked themselves. "We were idealistic, brimming with optimism—ready to tackle the apathy that infested our own schools and communities even as the political leaders at home and in Washington remained terminally unconvinced that a kid could make a difference."

The words come straight from a sweet, earnest book also entitled *Freedom's Answer* that was published in early 2004, written by a veritable rainbow coalition of students from across the country who, in their words, "begged each other not to forget what happened when they dared to dream." The sentiment hits you like a red-white-and-blue ice pop on a steamy Fourth of July—a soothing, sugary antidote to a confused world. No one can fault the intentions of this group, which encourages students to organize at their schools by seeking ten voting pledges per person, and then "delivering" them on Election Day. Freedom's Answer students also promise to stand outside "every voting booth in America" to thank those who cared enough about the franchise to use it.

"We think of it as the most powerful civics lesson that could be taught," Doug Bailey explains. "It is not a homework assignment or a project with parents hovering over every detail—it is a student-owned movement to empower a new generation. They learn not just the power of one vote, they learn that they as a generation have the power to change the political system if they don't like it."

Bravo! My only question is whether wrapping this crusade in the tattered flag of the September 11 terrorist attacks is the best way to reach young voters. Freedom's Answer isn't the only civic organization that relies heavily on the emotion and patriotism generated that day to connect. A moving video from the Close-Up Foundation used in classrooms across America interviews students from a school just blocks away from the devastation in lower Manhattan. Perhaps the framers of these messages see something I am missing. True, the attacks and all that has come since have already profoundly shaped the nation that young people will inherit—from the size of the federal budget to the nature of our foreign policy to the lines at airports. But this was not Pearl Harbor and the start of years of sacrifice and war. This was, thankfully, a onetime experience. And this was not an attack on our government; the targets were the emblems of our commercial and military might. Except for those directly affected by the horror at the Twin Towers, the Pentagon, and a field in western Pennsylvania, except for those who lost a loved one or a home or a way of life, young Americans' daily existence has not been transformed by this event. All the polls prove this. In fact, the polls show that terrorism is, for young people, a notch below education and the economy when it comes to issues they wish government to address.

Freedom's Answer bases its appeal on "the amazing acts of heroism" following the attacks, directing that energy now to mobilizing the vote. Like the other nonpartisan efforts, it steers clear of political talk, relying instead on the pure passion of its volunteers and their ability to surprise an indifferent public. It claims to have generated "the largest voter turnout for a non-presidential election in U.S. history," a claim that we'll let history resolve. History will no doubt also have a say over whether September 11 can, indeed, become a rallying cry for a new generation. However the message is delivered, though, the thousands of young people moved to join this fledgling, dynamic effort are proof of a hunger out there to be agents of change. "For roughly twenty years a generation of young Americans have opted out of the political system—mostly out of cynicism, not apathy," says Bailey. "Our goal at Freedom's Answer is to get a new generation to opt back in."

* * *

Other national efforts also bear mention. The National Student/Parent Mock Election does what its name suggests: encourages students and their parents to participate in a presidential campaign by discussing the issues and then voting as if it were the real thing. It is run by a network of volunteers at no charge to the participating schools, bolstered by free voter education materials and the use of a CNN webcast. One evaluation, by the University of Colorado, found that participating in the mock election increased the belief that voting is important and decreased the sense of powerlessness held by too many young people—and adults—when it comes to the voting process.

Playing pretend politics by itself is of questionable value. Americans are inundated with polls and surveys; they dot every website and are featured on many television shows. But like the mock party conventions that some high schools stage every four years, this national mock election provides a proper antidote to the personality-driven "voting" that too often grabs the attention of the American public. Issues are discussed, and the choices are more profound than picking which formerly unknown singer will get a new record contract.

Meantime, a small but growing number of entities are trying to increase youth voting by increasing the number of young people running for office, on the theory that the excitement and precedent of a fresh new campaign will excite a dormant electorate. I called the groups "entities" because some don't fit the traditional mold of an "organization" and wouldn't even exist were it not for the Internet.

Party Y, for instance, bills itself as a bold new twenty-first-century "all-partisan, virtual" party that exists solely for the purpose of encouraging, highlighting, and supporting anyone under thirty who runs for political office. And they mean anyone—including the six offbeat candidates who ran in California's 2003 gubernatorial recall free-for-all, among them a young man whose campaign was financed by his win on *Wheel of Fortune* and a twenty-three-year-old porn star who suggested that breast implants be taxed to pay off the state's deficit. Party Y claims to be led by their fearless leader and poster boy "Cousin Sam," the alleged illegitimate son of a geriatric Uncle Sam and an underage White House intern, discreetly delivered in a broom closet in the Oval Office and abandoned along a presidential campaign trail.

But seriously, Party Y notes that only one of the 435 seats in the House of Representatives is held by someone under thirty, and they'll use outrageous ideas to get young voters' attention. (A traveling pseudo-reality show following a young candidate is in the works.)

"Public service is the rent we pay for our time here on earth," says Party Y's cofounder, Thomas Bryer, a doctoral student in public administration at the University of Southern California in Los Angeles. "It's time for our generation to step up and lead us. What appears to be a failure of citizenship is a failure of political leadership. Our answer to the nonvoter is—if no one on the ballot excites you, run for office yourself. You need to enter the game and honor the spirit of the Constitution."

Cousin Sam is edgy and humorous, but VoterVirgin elicits an immediate smile, and that is its intent. Teresa Van Deusen was unemployed in Austin, Texas, when she came up with the idea in 2003, and took what little savings she had to launch this Web-based resource for anyone who wants to register voters. "We didn't want to re-create the wheel," she told the members of the Youth Vote Coalition. "You guys are putting the chips on the table. We're the salsa."

The idea was to be funny and not preachy, to turn on potential voters with a mobilization tool that would make men laugh and would at least draw a chuckle from women. Voter-Virgin offers a Registration Assistance Kit, pens and banners emblazoned with its mod purple and red logo, and encourages visitors to its website to send inspiring e-mail messages to nonvoters called "Spread the Love." Van Deusen acknowledges that there's no way to scientifically measure the effect of her idea, but you have to admire her pluck. "I think the nation is looking for a reason to smile and I am happy to be a part of that for such a good cause," she told me.

* * *

While there's no telling whether these whimsical entrepreneurial ventures will last through one election cycle, it's clear that the Internet is here to stay. Party Y and VoterVirgin, national mock elections, and Freedom's Answer—none of these enterprises could have existed even ten years ago, until cyberspace became the place to be for many young Americans.

The story of how the Internet's power to inform, connect, and mobilize young voters will shape the future of American politics is unfolding before us, and the narrative is promising. That might seem to contradict my strongly held belief that politics must become more personal, but in fact when used well— and that is a crucial caveat—the Internet can break down the isolation, alienation, and disengagement that keeps so many young people from voting. This is their medium. This is how they relate to the world, cheaply and quickly, rendering other forms of communication, commerce, and instruction obsolete. Ignoring it could be as foolish or as perilous a civic decision as ignoring the protests outside Capitol Hill in 1968.

But how to use the Internet? On-line voting is often proposed as an easy solution to the hassles of Election Day, and for college students especially, it has some appeal. Students are often on-line continuously, leaving "away messages" via Instant Messenger even if they are not in their dorm rooms. (Sometimes, this is the only way to know what our daughter in college is actually doing.) So ubiquitous is students' connection to the Internet that universities have found a sharp increase in voting for student government elections if they are held on-line.

Expanding that capability to real world elections is problematic, though. A profound "digital divide" still exists in America, leaving those with less education and lower income on the bumpy side road of the Internet highway. Besides, less than half of the nation's eighteen- to twenty-four-year-olds are in college, and it is unfair to create a new outlet for voting that would overly benefit the elites while requiring less advantaged young people to use the existing cumbersome, unfriendly system.

The most ambitious use of Internet voting to date took place in the Democratic presidential primary in Arizona in 2000, the first binding on-line balloting. In late February of that year, the party sent a voter certificate and a password to each of the state's 843,000 registered Democrats. During a four-day election window, voters logged on to a server with the PIN and two other forms of identification and, if the ID matched, could pick their presidential and congressional candidates from the privacy of their home computer room, at two in the morning, dressed in pajamas. (Mail balloting was also allowed.) The results were stunning: Turnout was up by more than 600 percent compared to the 1996 primary, and 41 percent of those who voted did so on-line. All in all, over 37,000 people cast ballots remotely, 20,000 more used mail-in ballots, and another 20,000 actually came to the polls, which were open for one day of conventional, in-person voting. Democratic Party officials contended that turnout was also substantially higher in predominately Native American and Latino areas than it was four years earlier, but the Voter Integrity Project still criticized the system as a modern form of the "literacy tests" that barred the poorly educated minority voters in the past.

Still, the concern about equal access is not the only worry with Internet voting; accountability is a serious issue with off-site balloting. Although the Help America Vote Act passed in the wake of the 2000 Florida voting debacle mandated that voters be able to verify their ballots before they are cast and counted, there is growing evidence that even conventional voting procedures using electronic machines are not dependable. How, then, can voters sending in their choices through the mail or through cyberspace be assured of an accurate, untampered count without a paper trail? They can't. In fact, a panel of security experts reported in January 2004 that a new $22 million system to allow soldiers and other Americans overseas to vote via the Internet was inherently unsecure and should be abandoned. (It later was.)

Even more important, voting on-line turns this essentially social civic exercise into a private, isolated act. It obliterates the wonder of Election Day, the activity in polling places and on the street, the serendipity of meeting neighbors and striking up conversation, the chance to mingle and mix. A communal ritual reinforces itself; you feel better about voting when you see other people entering the booth and closing the curtain, adding their voice to the public chorus choosing its leaders. That can't be replicated in cyberspace.

The Internet can, however, create political community in other ways. The simplest and most well-known is its capacity for fund-raising, which Democratic presidential aspirant Howard Dean employed for maximum impact in the 2004 campaign. His huge initial lead in raising money was fueled by individual donations of less than $100 on average from a vast number of people nationwide. Not only did this propel his status early in the race; it potentially made him accountable to a broader citizenry than the exclusive clubs of the richest contributors and the power levers of the party. Young people understand that in the old system, their individual votes don't count as much as those with money. In this new fund-raising world, however, contributions can be more equalized and so, potentially, can political power.

This isn't only true in presidential campaigns. Mark Strama

is one of those who believe the Internet may one day change the face of politics. Strama worked for Rock the Vote, cofounded an on-line registration service called NewVoter.com, then was a vice president of election.com, and now is running for state legislature in Texas, and may be the first candidate to have a full-time technology person on his campaign staff. His favorite example of the might of the Internet is not Arizona's election or Dean's campaign, but the way it was employed to raise funds for the Texas Democrats who fled the state in the summer of 2003 in a redistricting battle with the Republicans. Working with MoveOn.org, the party solicited people on-line for $30 contributions. "I thought we'd raise $100,000," Strama recalled. "We raised a million dollars in forty-eight hours. I have seen it. It is powerful."

Beyond fund-raising, the Internet has shown its ability to create community and attract young people in the idiosyncratic Dean campaign. Popular political campaigns have long been magnets for young people aching to get involved, but usually their role is as functionary to the adult decision makers. Not so with the Dean campaign. Shunning the traditional hierarchy, this campaign sprung up in unlikely places—there were more than nine hundred *unofficial* Dean groups—through the use of Meetup.com, a free Internet service that organizes local gatherings "about anything, anywhere." Here's one example from a December 20, 2003, story in the *New York Times*:

> *"The first meet-ups were just three or four people who'd met on the Web," recalled Deb McCarver, a public relations specialist who has become co-chairwoman of Nashville for Dean. "People came, but we really didn't have an agenda. We said, what do people do in a political campaign? No one really had a clue."*

The campaign headquarters in Burlington, Vermont, urged the fledgling groups to do "some sort of event to increase Dean's visibility." So on their own, they'd leaflet a neighborhood, hold a rally, urge donations to the Dean campaign instead of holiday gift-giving. For a time, the Dean interactive website, Blog for America, got more than 40,000 hits a day; many supporters said it was the first thing they checked every morning. No one needed permission to undertake an activity on the candidate's behalf, and this unstructured freedom appealed especially to the young, who relished the chance to exert the kind of power that would never be theirs in a more conventional campaign. In this way, the Internet operates as a kind of cyber-matchmaker, enabling a political community to birth itself. On DeanLink, supporters could check out each other's photographs and interests online; using Get Local software, supporters could plan local gatherings and even download fliers independent of the central campaign.

While the Dean campaign may have been the most visible user of the Internet in the 2004 primaries, others before him pioneered its use to capture the attention of young people. Tammy Baldwin ran for Congress in 1988 for a seat representing the fairly liberal college town of Madison, Wisconsin, and the suburban and rural areas around it. Full-time students made up more than 10 percent of her district, and she used them to great advantage. Her campaign website devoted an entire section to students, and she sent out electronic newsletters frequently, advertising youth rallies and organized events. Thousands of students volunteered for her campaign, walking precincts, stuffing envelopes, manning phone banks, and agreeing to serve as "student captains" in the University's residence halls. Helped by Wisconsin's same-day registration, voter turnout was impressive, and some polling places even ran out of ballots. Now in her third term in Congress, Baldwin maintains a "student page" on her congressional website, still sends out electronic newsletters, and has a special "kids" section geared for the crowd not yet old enough to vote.

The same year Baldwin was elected Wisconsin's first woman representative, a burly wrestler was making his own political history next door in Minnesota. With little money but lots of name recognition, Jesse Ventura confounded the political establishment by using the Internet to organize the independent voters, especially young men, who were key to his gubernatorial victory, the first ever by a Reform Party candidate nationwide. His campaign's ambitious closing event—a 72-hour drive through Minnesota—was coordinated entirely by e-mail and through his Internet team, affectionately called the "Geek Squad." (Now that his stint in the governor's mansion has ended, Ventura fans can still use the Internet to purchase Jesse Ventura Bobblehead Dolls.)

The Internet will have to do more than act as a sophisticated phone chain or an on-line shopping network to truly create a political culture attractive to younger voters, and there's some evidence that an on-line youth civic culture is taking root. A report released in March 2004 by American University's Center for Social Media reveals that young people are going on-line to register to vote and volunteer, launch projects for community improvement, and learn skills for political action. Another new site launched for the 2004 election, youth04.org, uses the Internet to, in its words, "create a relationship between young voters and candidates for political office, from the President on down. We aim to motivate both sides of the relationship to listen to each other." The word *relationship* appears in bold face, to highlight its importance.

And that's what is needed. A new relationship.

* * *

Ryan Friedrichs believes that one way to create that relationship, to bring some romance and excitement to voting, is to ignite the old flame of partisanship. "The nonpartisan efforts will never actually move the numbers nationally," he says. "We need a sea change in the political world. We need the partisan community to believe they really need to do this."

Friedrichs is a product of what might be called the engaged Democratic left, but his passion for giving young people a *reason* to vote is shared by some of his political opponents, too, who are busily organizing college conservatives on campuses from Bucknell to Berkeley. The College Republican National Committee, a group that mobilizes students to campaign, has tripled its membership since 1999 to an all-time high of nearly 1,500 chapters and has geared up an impressive drive for the student vote in 2004.

Like the use of the Internet, this trend at first seems counterintuitive. If the sharp partisanship of politics turns off so many young people, if their dislike of the two-party system grows with each election, why look to those same institutions for salvation?

It took Friedrichs a few years to answer that question, years spent as a campus activist at the University of Michigan and then as the national field director for the Youth Vote Coalition, where he was continually haunted by whether even the "personal ask" mattered. "I didn't think it was enough," he said, so he went back to Harvard's Kennedy School of Government for a master's degree and a chance to investigate a hunch: that there was a cost-effective, measurable way for political campaigns to talk to young people and get them to vote. The Youth Coordinated Campaign used randomized experiments during the 2002 Michigan election on behalf of the state Democratic Party to test out three tactics: placing a tag with campaign information on the doors of potential voters aged eighteen to thirty-five; phoning them before Election Day; and striking up front door conversations.

Fourteen thousand door knocks, 24,000 phone calls, and 60,000 door hangers later, Friedrichs discovered that the more personal tactics had the highest impact and were the most cost effective. To wit: Door hangers increased turnout by 1 percent at a rate of $23 a vote. Volunteer phone calls boosted turnout by 2.5 percent and cost $8 a vote. Door-to-door conversations drove 10 percent more young people to the polls, at a rate of $10 a vote. Plus, he found that turnout was higher if the volunteers' message contained information on where to vote, polling hours, etc.

Sometimes you need gigantic, randomized studies to confirm what common sense would say all along. Make it personal, give them a reason to vote and ample information on how to do it, and they will, indeed, show up to pull that lever. It helped the Democrats in Michigan that a charismatic woman gubernatorial candidate topped their ticket that year. It helped Friedrichs's research that his party won.

Nonetheless, his "take-away" message is powerful: "It's Madonna on the TV to get their attention, to make it cool, but then as soon as she's off, it's someone knocking on the door, asking them to vote. It's the combination. You need a local face, a local message. You need to have the parties and you need to have the candidates."

* * *

Mostly, we need the collective will to help young people rediscover the importance of political power and the obligation to use it wisely. The individual will, the inspiring anecdotes, are everywhere. During the course of researching this book, I found that sometimes the simplest ideas made the most sense and struck at the heart of what is missing from our political culture.

In Woodbury, New Jersey, school superintendent Judy Wilson told me that overall turnout for the local school board election in her community nearly doubled the year that the incumbents and challengers agreed to speak in high school social studies classes. "Students felt a direct impact on their school and its future, recognized their influence and power in the community and moved into action within their families and neighborhoods," she says. "When the issues and people were both close and real to their lives, students were eager to be involved."

Why don't we involve students in school board elections? They're experts on the subject, and even if they're about to graduate, what happens in schools will affect their younger siblings, neighbors, and teachers. It doesn't get more personal than that. As the Woodbury example shows, there could be a profound "trickle-up" effect, encouraging other family members to vote, too. Besides, for a generation accustomed to immediate results, local races offer a chance to more readily see the effect of one vote than a mammoth, national contest.

Another story: At Wissahickon High School in suburban Philadelphia, members of the local Blue Bell Rotary Club committed themselves to reversing the declining voter trends with a simple, effective program that should be hosted in every school in the country. Four to six times a year, they set up a table in the school cafeteria at lunchtime and wait as designated student leaders make the rounds and cajole their friends to come up and register. The combination of a peer "ask" and assistance from seasoned adults has resulted in 80 percent of Wissahickon's student body registered before graduation. (They're hoping for 100 percent.) The Rotarians also sponsor an education program with local elected officials and arrange to bring voting machines into the building for the annual senior class elections. As Rotarian Richard Schwarz Jr. said, "Our message is simple: As young Americans, you have earned the right to have a voice and to help determine your future. Reaching eighteen and not voting is like working hard to earn a paycheck and not cashing it."

Why don't schools pledge that every eligible young American will be registered to vote before receiving a high school diploma? Each community can decide how and when to do the registration drive, whether to enlist the Rotarians or the wrestlers or homegrown celebrities; the details are immaterial, it's the commitment that counts. While it is true that registration isn't enough, that voting is both a habit *and* a cause, the involvement of every school in every community telegraphs an unmistakable statement of values to young people. It's no secret that American schools are eager to sponsor winning sports teams. Why can't they be just as eager to develop active citizens?

And, as long as I'm asking simple questions, why can't every high school student spend at least part of Election Day at a polling place, witnessing real democracy in action?

I assigned that task to my students at the University of Pennsylvania, and the results astonished even them. Granted, the city of Philadelphia was playing host to a controversial mayor's race in November 2003 that was more captivating than the first season of *The West Wing*. Still, Dan Zavodnick bluntly confessed that he thought hard about how to get out of this assignment. "I was not looking forward to standing around for three hours, waiting to bother busy people as they tried to get back to their lives," he wrote afterward. "I never thought I could elicit any worthwhile insights by asking one simple question. To this end, I spent the morning of Nov. 4, 2003, thinking of ways I could convince myself that it was all right to stay for ten minutes.... I want to sincerely thank you, professor. I have to say that my four hours outside Ward 27, Division 1 at 4247 Locust Street were the most interesting, enlightening and fun academic hours of my Penn experience."

And this from a senior majoring in political science.

What so moved Zavodnick? He approached voters of all ages, especially the young, and asked why they voted; the range of answers, not all of them inspiring, provided a reality check on what was, until then, an entirely theoretical experience of politics and community life. He saw one young woman dash out of the polling place, jubilantly cheering and shouting as she ran down the street because she had voted for the very first time. He spoke to another who claimed that "all the candidates suck." As you can tell, this assignment was not scripted by the League of Women Voters; it was messy, frustrating, demoralizing, and even ugly. Jimmy Christianson was shocked by the violence at some polling places—there were over fifty reported incidents citywide that day—and the shrugging acceptance of many Philadelphia voters of the inevitability that somebody, somewhere, is gonna get hit. Christianson was horrified by a bureaucracy so impenetrable that some newly registered residents gave up and left without voting. And because this was Philadelphia, he also encountered one voter who was registered in two different locations. "If things like this happened in a Third World nation, Americans would be appalled and believe that the election should be held again," he wrote.

Other students emerged with a far more positive, inspiring picture. Chun Shin, who emigrated to the United States with his family from Korea, had only been a citizen for three years and, unlike the other students in the class, knew of no one who voted here for the first time in 1972. His impression of American elections was still largely blank. On that morning, the weather warm and inviting, he filled in the spaces by talking to young voters of all races, motivations, and persuasions as he rode his bicycle through west and north Philadelphia. "The answers to why these young voters came out to vote were consistent: it was their duty to vote, their votes counted, and issues were important," he wrote. "I felt like, in this overly individualistic society, these people understood the inherent and undeniable interconnectedness among individuals.... They seemed like they had a purpose in what they were doing."

The fact that young people voted for so many varied and

sometimes conflicting reasons—duty, ideology, issues, pay-back, family tradition, or just because—was a revelation to these students, as was the fact that many took this act of citizenship so seriously. "I never anticipated the extent to which everyone involved in the voting process valued their right to participate," wrote Deirdre Connolly, a civic agnostic until then. "From this experience alone I've realized that the voting process is qualitatively different than volunteering and community service, and choosing one won't fulfill one's civic responsibilities."

Connolly saw some hot-tempered behavior that day, too, but to her it reflected the passion and importance of the election. There is no currency in seeking to sugarcoat this experience. Young people must see the process in all its glory and with all its flaws, so redolent of human nature, so essential to personal identity and the community's future welfare.

"If every potential young voter were required to survey other young voters at polling sites, I think our tragically low turnout would be a thing of the past," Connolly believes. "This was truly eye-opening for someone like me, who has never ridden the voting wave to the polls. Despite the controversies and incidents of what must have been an anomalous Election Day, or maybe because of them, I was inspired by the patriotism shown by the least likely of individuals and felt the allure of inclusion in a group whose only membership card is that of citizenship."

*   *   *

Finally, I'd like to introduce an idea of my own into the mix of possible ways to get young people to vote. The First Vote ritual is a modest attempt to change civic culture incrementally and to function, in the best tradition of ritual, as a social statement of values.

The idea for the ritual came to me after the epiphany of the

May 2002 primary, when I realized that my daughter's First Vote went largely unnoticed and I decided that neglect of this moment should no longer be an option. The concept is simple, inexpensive, and easily adapted: Parents, teachers, coaches, clergy and other caring adults should create a First Vote ritual to publicly acknowledge this civic coming-of-age each Election Day. How?

• High schools can announce the names of students who have cast a First Vote over the loud speaker at morning announcements, or from the stage at a school assembly.

• Colleges can publish the names of First Voters in the campus newspapers.

• Clergy can announce their names from the pulpit the following week.

• Public officials can send First Voters letters of congratulations.

• Schools can offer them free entrance to the next football game or dance party.

• Restaurants could give them a free cup of coffee.

• Radio stations can read out their names and interview them on air.

Most important, families can celebrate this achievement by presenting their new citizen with a book or some other token to remember the occasion. Or take him out for pizza. Or buy her flowers. The intent is not to create yet another shopping opportunity or retailing event for Hallmark, but to demonstrate the value of the vote with at least the passion and purpose we bring to highlighting our children's academic, athletic, and artistic accomplishments. By acknowledging the First Vote, by making a public fuss, we can demonstrate to a generation wary of hype and manipulation that they are, indeed, a welcome and necessary part of our democracy.

There is a slender, historical justification for this type of celebration. On May 3, 1940, President Roosevelt approved a congressional resolution that set aside the third Sunday in May as a public occasion to recognize all who, by coming of age or by naturalization, attained the status of citizen. Far as I can tell, this splendid idea was swallowed up by the nation's relentless appetite for all things military in the wake of World War II. By 1949, the third Saturday of May was declared Armed Forces Day, and that Sunday was consigned to be the bookmark at the end of Armed Forces Week.

The analogy isn't perfect, true. Attaining the "status of citizen" is a vague phrase, and voting a concrete act. I'm not sure yet whether another holiday in May will do anything to buff up America's civic body.

But I appreciate the sentiment. Just imagine if today our political, cultural, educational, and religious leaders urged the nation to celebrate a young person's First Vote as a rite of passage and the rest of us took up the call, infusing this ancient act with new meaning and shoring up the democracy our children will inherit.

Acknowledgments

This book was written with the support of the Robert A. Fox Leadership Program at the University of Pennsylvania, a powerhouse of energy and idealism seeking to teach the qualities of civic leadership inside and outside the classroom. As a senior fellow since 2002, and a fellow in residence during the 2003–2004 academic year, I have enjoyed working with Chuck Brutsche, Christy Bunner, Feather Houstoun, Mark Alan Hughes, Sheria Sellers-Crawley, Mary Summers, and Camille Washington. Special thanks goes to Joseph Tierney for so wisely responding to my thoughts and worries, and to the incomparable John J. DiIulio Jr., whose kindness, devotion, intelligence, and patriotism I will always admire.

To paraphrase an ancient Jewish saying, I have learned much wisdom from my teachers, more from my colleagues, and most from my students—in this case, the members of PSCI-298, who studied with me in the fall of 2003. Most are mentioned by name in the text, but since they all contributed mightily to the work, I want to credit them individually. Thank you to Jimmy Christianson, Deirdre Connolly, Ben Cruse, Adelia Hwang, Dan Koken, Rachel Kreinces, Kate Liberman, Michael Schimmel, Chun Shin, Blake Stuchin, Paul Townsend, Nick Walters, Marc Williams, Erin Wilson, and Dan Zavodnick.

I have spent nearly a quarter-century, most of my professional life, at the *Philadelphia Inquirer*, as a reporter, foreign correspondent, editor, and now as a columnist. Journalism is a cumulative endeavor, and if you are smart (or lucky, or both), one assignment informs another, so that no experience ever need be wasted. Thus was my passion for civic life nurtured, from the time I covered the Trenton statehouse as a young reporter, to the years when I was in charge of navigating the editorial board through the thicket of major local and national crises. Many of the ideas expressed in this book were first explored in my columns, and I thank the *Inquirer* for allowing me to bring them to fuller existence here. Through it all, the support of my editors and newsroom colleagues never wavered. I am especially indebted to my current editors and longtime friends John Timpane and Chris Satullo, whose intellect, creativity, and impeccable civic values have improved my work beyond measure.

I also wish to acknowledge E. J. Dionne Jr. and The Brookings Institution for including some of these ideas in two of their publications, *Community Works: The Revival of Civil Society in America* (1998) and *United We Serve: National Service and the Future of Citizenship* (2003).

I extend my deep gratitude to Barbara Rifkind of the Barbara Rifkind Literary Agency for all she did to help birth this book, and to Joanne Wyckoff and the other wonderful people at Beacon Press for their fine editing and counsel.

Finally, I wish to thank my family, the entire Eisner/Berger/Zucker clan, for their unending love and support, and especially my sister and father for their steadfast belief in this project and my mother, for being there in her own way. When we were young, my sister and I used to jokingly complain that our parents, as ordinary working Americans, weren't well connected enough to help us in our chosen fields of journalism and public service. I understand now that they gave us exactly what we needed: a childhood filled with concern for the world around us, and with adults willing to engage and debate. Not only around our dinner table were these values expressed, but at family gatherings with an uncle who loved to argue, and at synagogue with a rabbi known for eloquent sermons on social justice. It's taken decades of research to prove what our parents instinctively knew was the best way to raise citizens of character.

This book—this cause, really—is dedicated to my three daughters, Rachel, Amalia, and Miriam. For the joy and privilege of being their mother, and for all else good in my life, I give thanks to my husband, Mark Berger, for his strength, love, and encouragement, and his inexhaustible supply of back rubs.

Sources

BOOKS

Boyers, Sarah Jane. *Teen Power Politics*. Brookfield, Conn.: The Millwood Press, 2000.

Cultice, Wendell W. *Youth's Battle for the Ballot* Westport, Conn.: Greenwood Press, 1992.

Cuomo, Andrew, ed. *Crossroads: The Future of American Politics*. New York: Random House, 2003.

Howe, Neil and William Strauss. *Millennials Rising: The Next Great Generation*. New York: Vintage Books, 2000.

Keyssar, Alexander. *The Right to Vote: The Contested History of Democracy in the United States*. New York: Basic Books, 2000.

Patterson, Thomas E. *The Vanishing Voter: Public Involvement in an Age of Uncertainty*. New York: Alfred A. Knopf, 2002.

Perry, James L., and Ann Marie Thomson. *Civic Service: What Difference Does It Make?* New York: M. E. Sharpe, Inc., 2004.

Putnam, Robert D. *Bowling Alone, The Collapse and Revival of American Community*. New York: Simon & Schuster, 2000.

Putnam, Robert D., and Lewis M. Feldstein. *Better Together: Restoring the American Community*. New York: Simon & Schuster, 2003.

Schudson, Michael. *The Good Citizen: A History of American Civic Life*. Cambridge, Mass.: Harvard University Press, 1999.

Sitaraman, Ganesh, and Previn Warren. *Invisible Citizens: Youth Politics After September 11*. Lincoln, Neb.: iUniverse, Inc., 2003.

Skocpol, Theda. *Diminished Democracy: From Membership to Management in American Civic Life*. University of Oklahoma Press, 2003.

The September 11 Generation. *Freedom's Answer*. Beverly Hills, Calif.: Little Moose Press, 2003.

Wilson, James Q., and John J. DiIulio Jr. *American Government*, 9th ed. Boston: Houghton Mifflin, 2004.

RESEARCH RESOURCES ON VOTING
AND CIVIC ENGAGEMENT

Carnegie Corporation of New York
437 Madison Ave.
New York, NY 10022
212-371-3200
www.carnegie.org

Center for Democracy and Citizenship
1301 K St. NW, Suite 450 West
Washington, D.C. 20005
202-728-0418
www.campaignyoungvoters.org

CIRCLE: Center for Information and Research
on Civic Learning and Engagement
School of Public Affairs
University of Maryland
College Park, MD 20742
301-405-2790
www.civicyouth.org

Committee for the Study of the American Electorate
601 Pennsylvania Ave. NW
Washington, D.C. 20004
202-546-3221
csnag@erols.com

Harvard University Institute of Politics
79 JFK Street
Cambridge, MA 02138
617-495-1360
www.iop.harvard.edu

International Institute for Democracy
and Electoral Assistance
Stromsborg, S-103 34
Stockholm, Sweden
www.idea.int

National Center for Learning and Citizenship
The Panetta Institute
100 Campus Center, Building 86E
California State University, Monterey Bay
Seaside, California 93955
831-582-4200
www.panettainstitute.org

Youth Vote Coalition
1010 Vermont Ave. NW
Washington, D.C. 20005
202-783-4751
www.youthvote.org

OTHER USEFUL WEB ADDRESSES

Center for Civic Education: www.civiced.org

Choose or Lose: www.mtv.com/news/chooseorlose

Close-up Foundation: www.closeup.org

Declare Yourself: www.declareyourself.com

Freedom's Answer: www.freedomsanswer.net

Hip Hop Summit Action Network:
www.hiphopsummitactionnetwork.org

Kids Voting USA: www.kidsvotingusa.org

National Student/Parent Mock Election:
www.nationalmockelection.org

New Voters Project: www.newvotersproject.org

Party Y: www.party-y.org

Rock the Vote: www.rockthevote.org

Smackdown Your Vote!: www.smackdownyourvote.com

Student Voices: www.student-voices.org

United Leaders: www.unitedleaders.org

USA Freedom Corps: www.usafreedomcorps.gov

VoterVirgin: www.votervirgin.com

Youth Service America: www.SERVEnet.org

Youth04.org: www.youth04.org